I Heard You Can Draw ©

Farm Animals!
(and more)

A step-by-step drawing guide

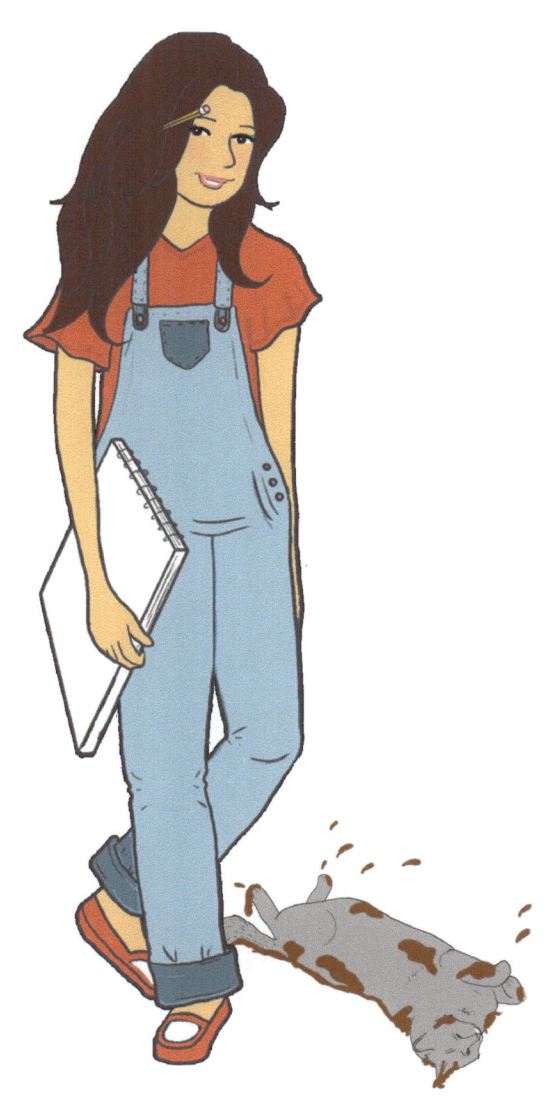

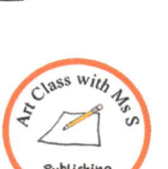

Art Class with Ms S Books

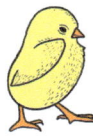

This book is for all of the kids
out there who love to draw!

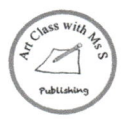

Art Class with Ms S

ISBN-10: 0989649075
ISBN-13: 978-0-9896490-7-0

BISAC: Juvenile Nonfiction / Art / Drawing

I Heard You Can Draw ©

Farm Animals!
(and more)

A step-by-step drawing guide

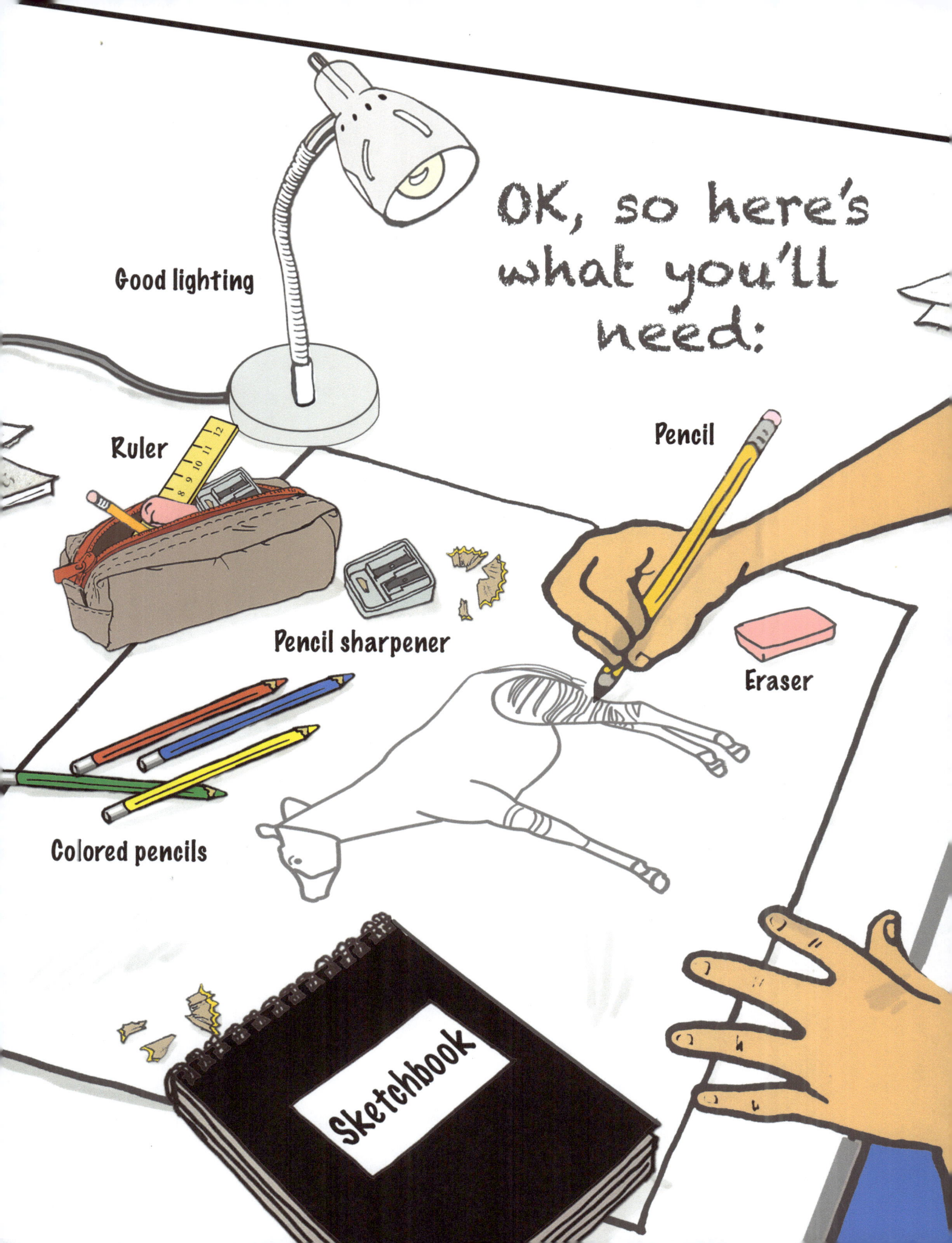

Did you know that when you draw

you are using the Elements of Art?

The Elements of Art:

Color
(Color is seen when light reflects off of an object)

Red Orange Yellow
Green Blue Indigo Violet

Line
(Has length and width)

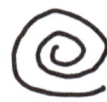
Spiral

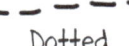
Dotted

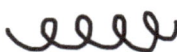
Curly

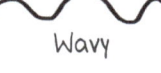
Wavy

Zig Zag

Straight

Shape
(A 2-D closed line)

Form
(Something three-dimensional)

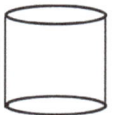
Cylinder

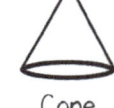
Cone

Cube

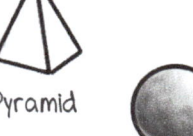
Objects

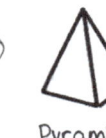
Pyramid

Sphere

Texture
(The way something feels)

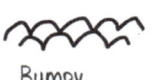
Bumpy

Rough →

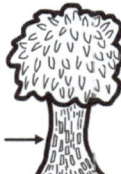

Sharp

Space
(Showing the distance between and around things)

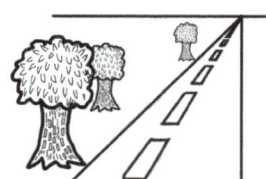

Value
(The darks and lights of your drawing)

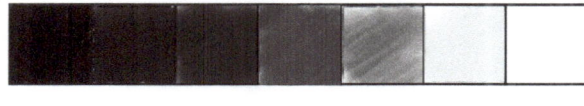

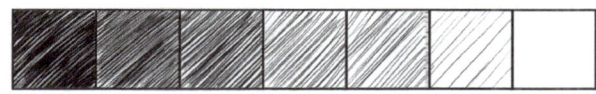

I Heard You Can Draw a...
Chicken!

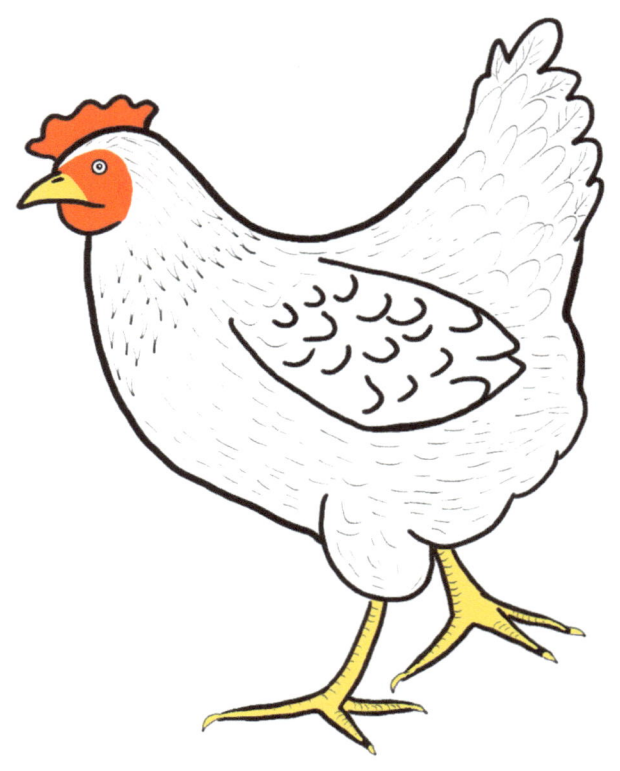

Chickens are birds. Female chickens are called hens,
male chickens are called roosters and their babies
are called chicks. Female chickens lay eggs.
Did you notice that chickens have a red comb on their heads?

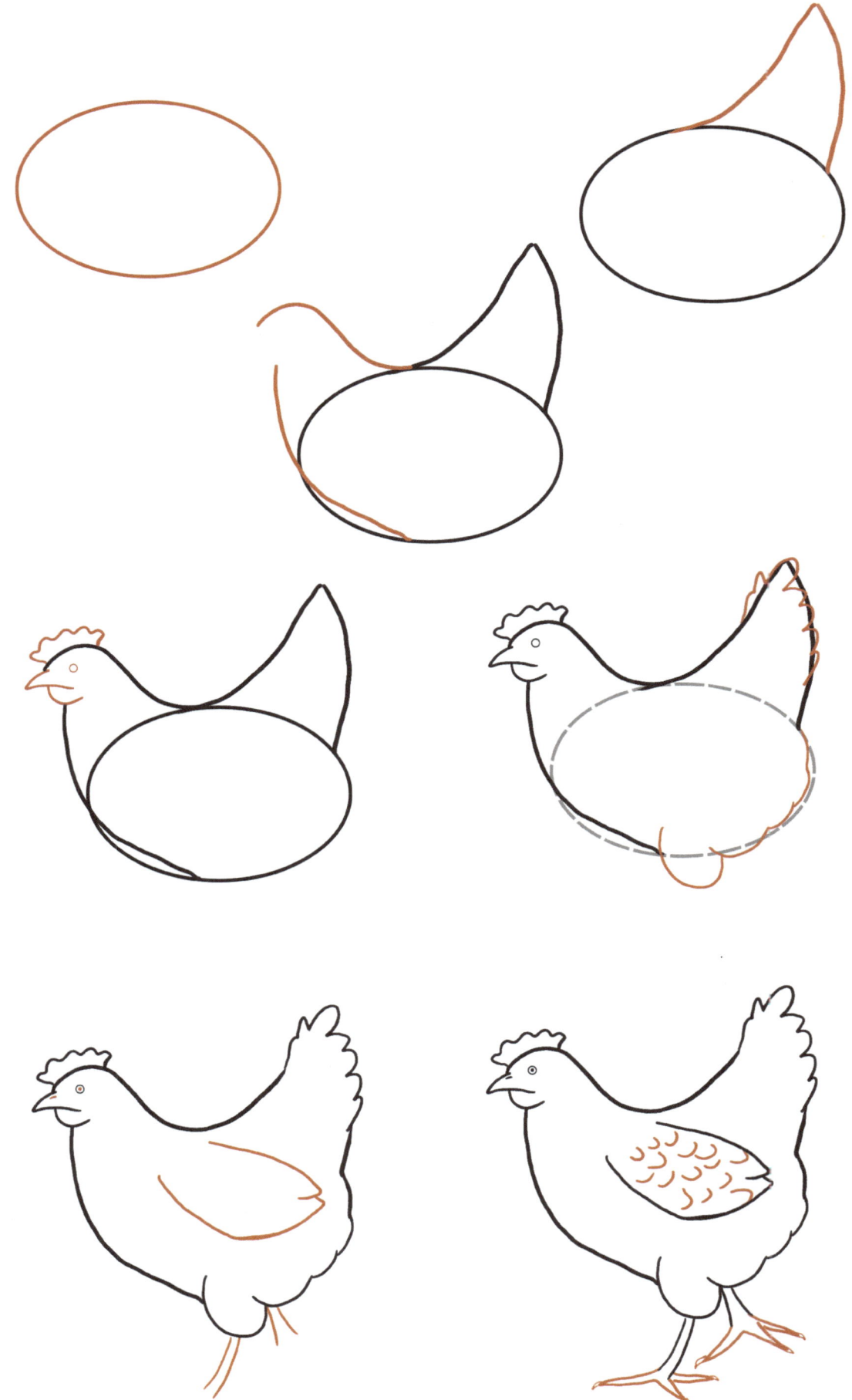

I Heard You Can Draw a...
Rooster!

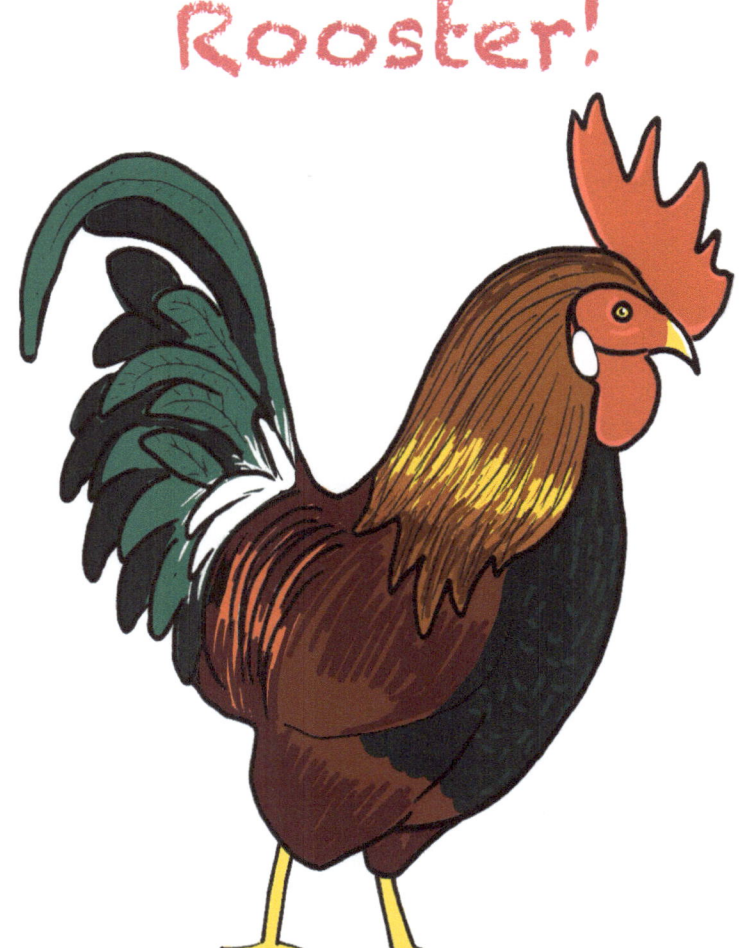

Roosters are male chickens. They are larger and more colorful than hens. They have a red comb on the top of their heads and a wattle under their chins.

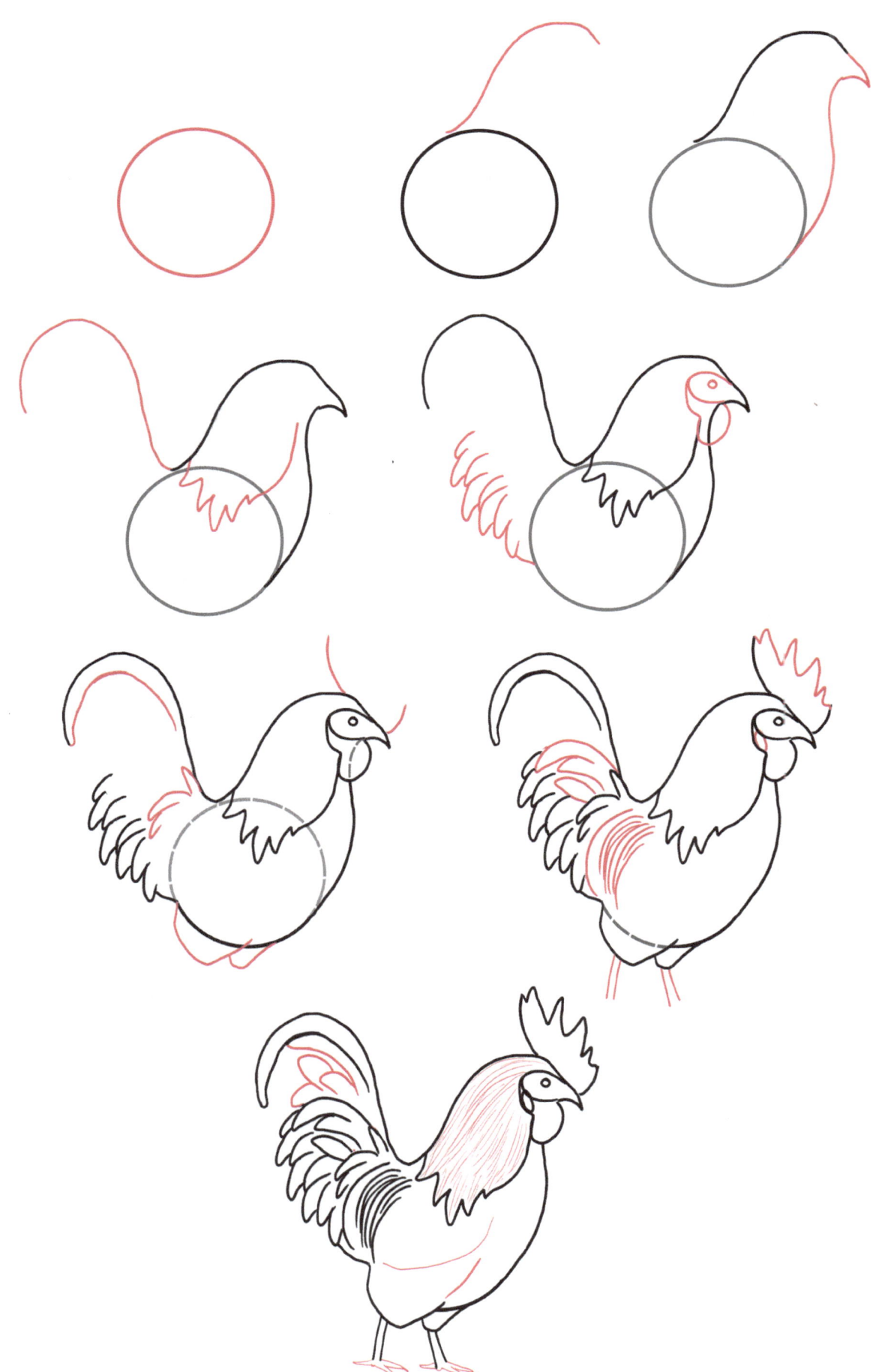

I Heard You Can Draw a...
Chick!

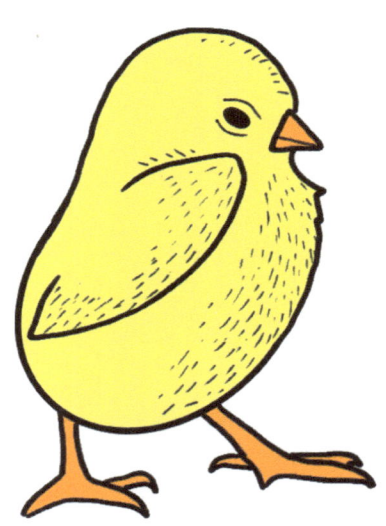

Chicks are baby chickens. They hatch out of an egg.
Before they hatch, a hen will sit on her eggs to keep them warm!

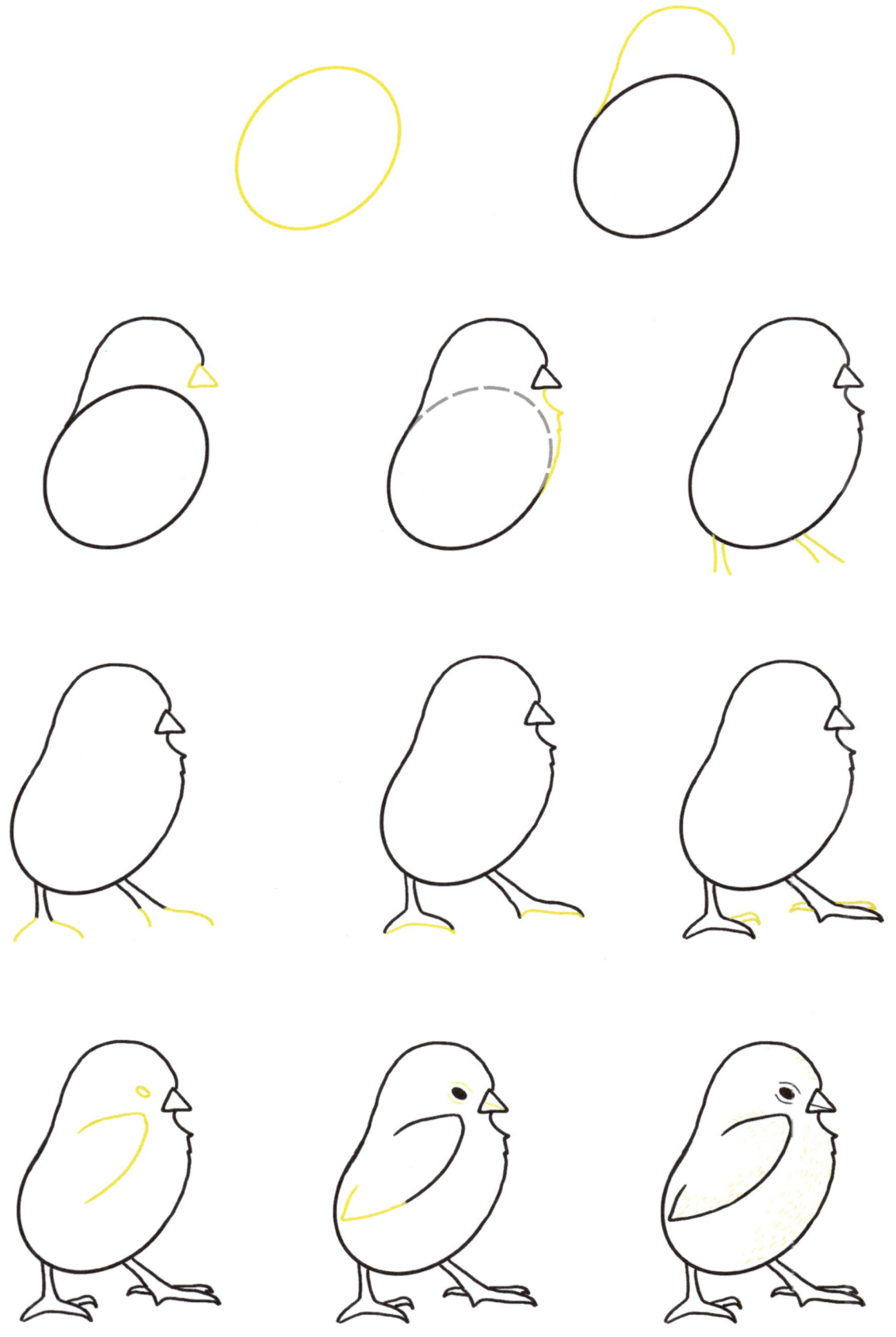

I Heard You Can Draw an...
American Quarter Horse!

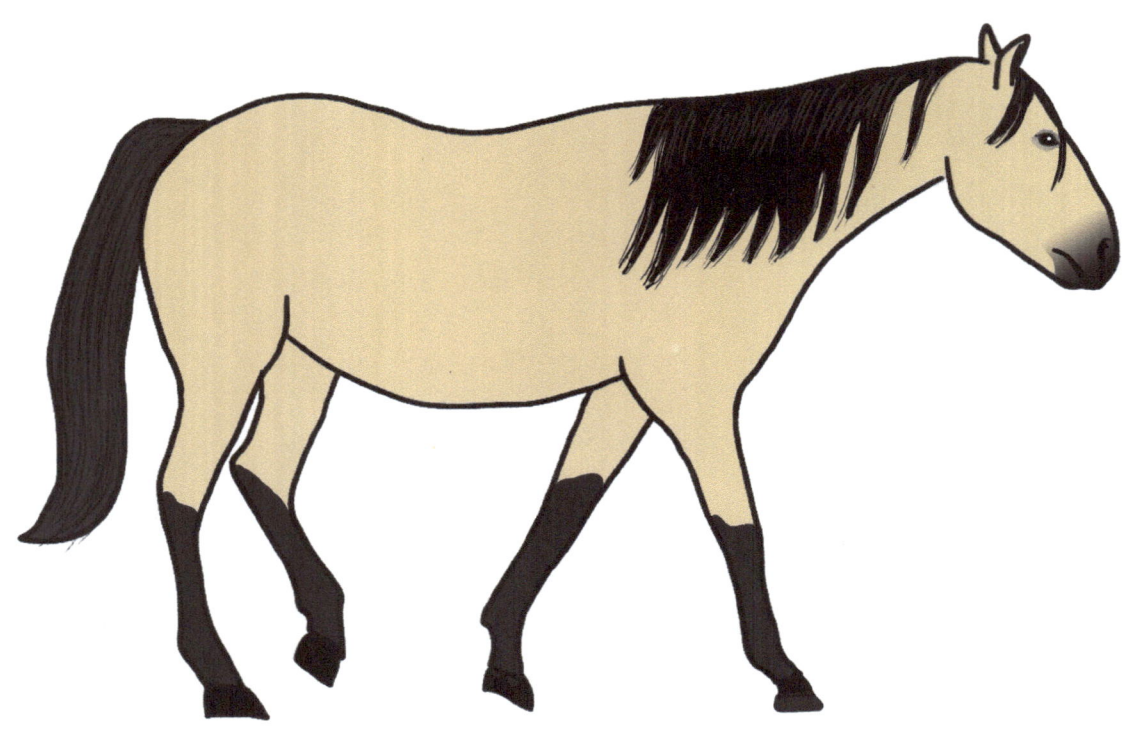

A male horse is called a stallion, a female horse is called a mare.
Baby horses are called foals. Baby male horses are called colts
and baby female horses are called fillies.
Horses are herbivores which means that they eat plants.

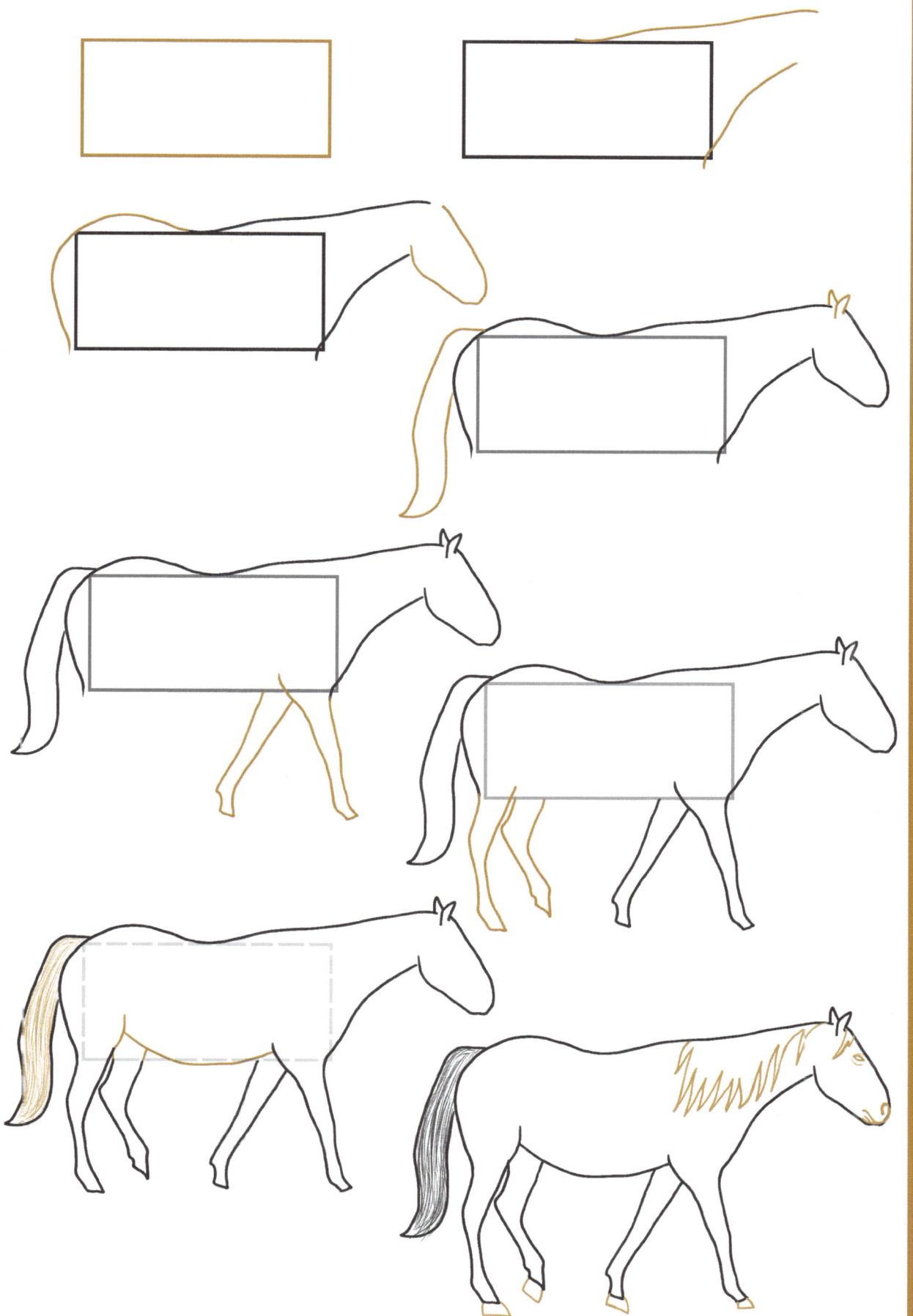

I Heard You Can Draw a...
Pony!

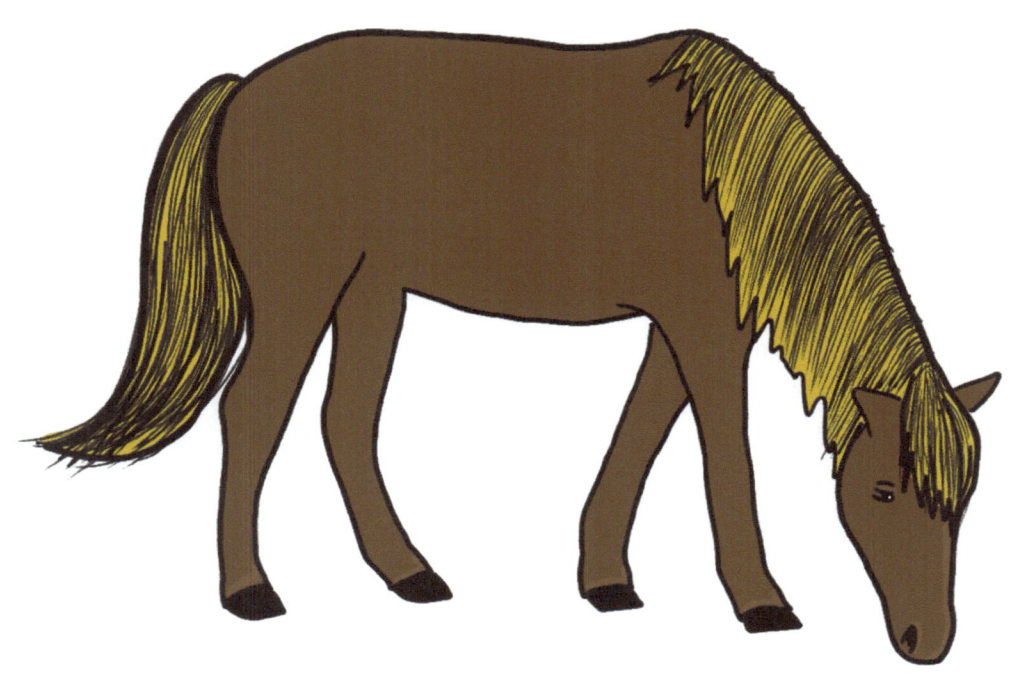

A pony is a small horse. Horses live in groups called herds. Horses have eyes on the sides of their head so they can see almost all the way around them.

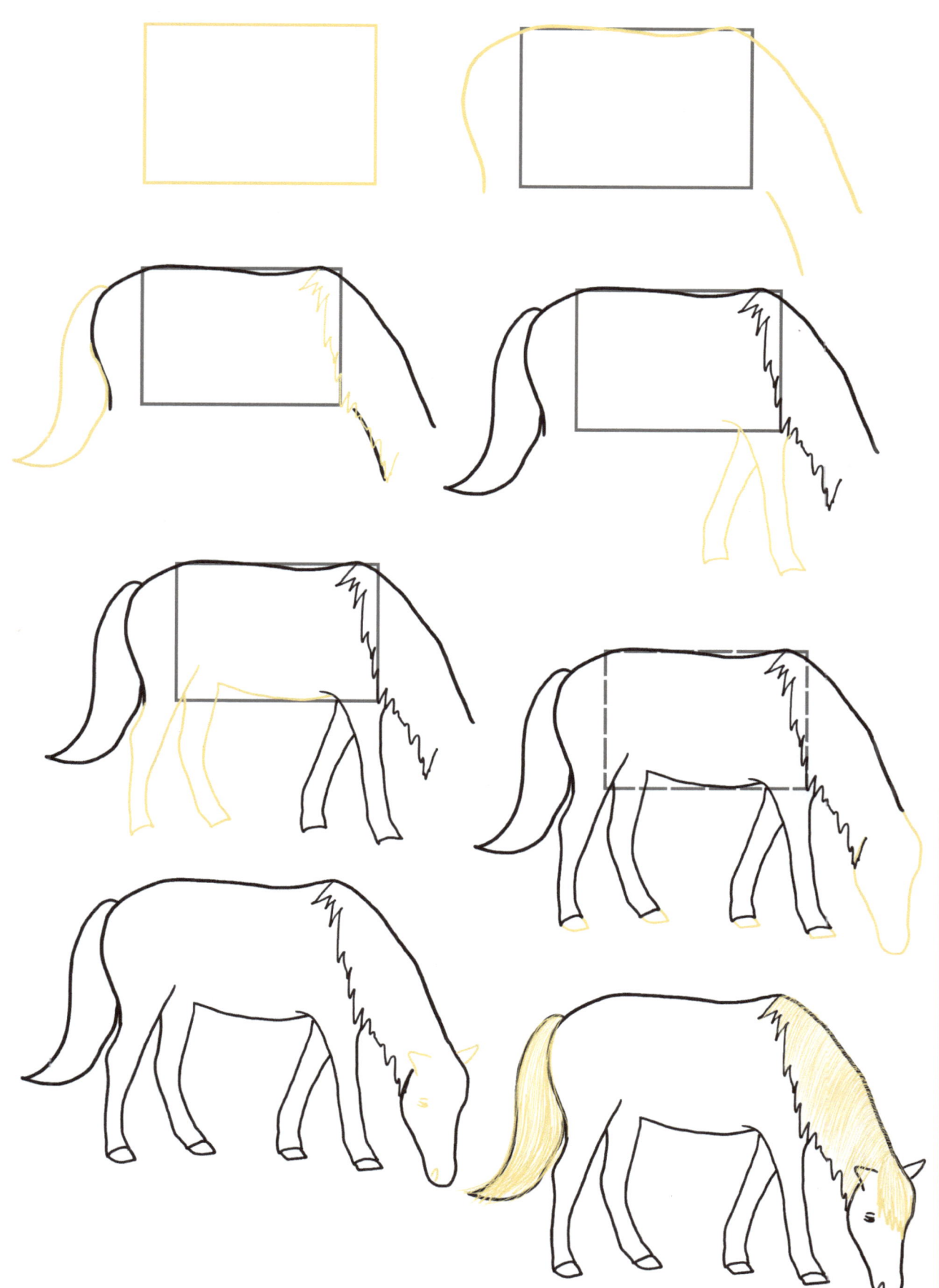

I Heard You Can Draw a...
Sheep!

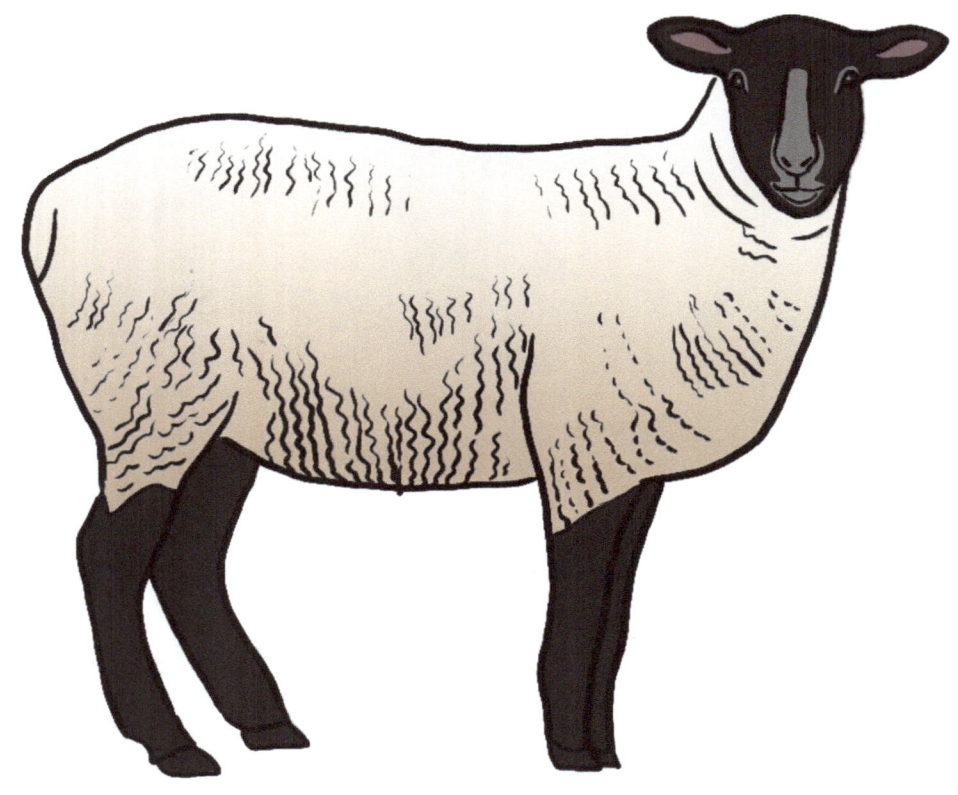

Sheep live on farms. Their fleece, or their coat, is used to make wool. They only eat plants and they live in groups called flocks. Adult female sheep are called ewes (ewe sounds like "you"), adult males are called rams and their babies are called lambs.

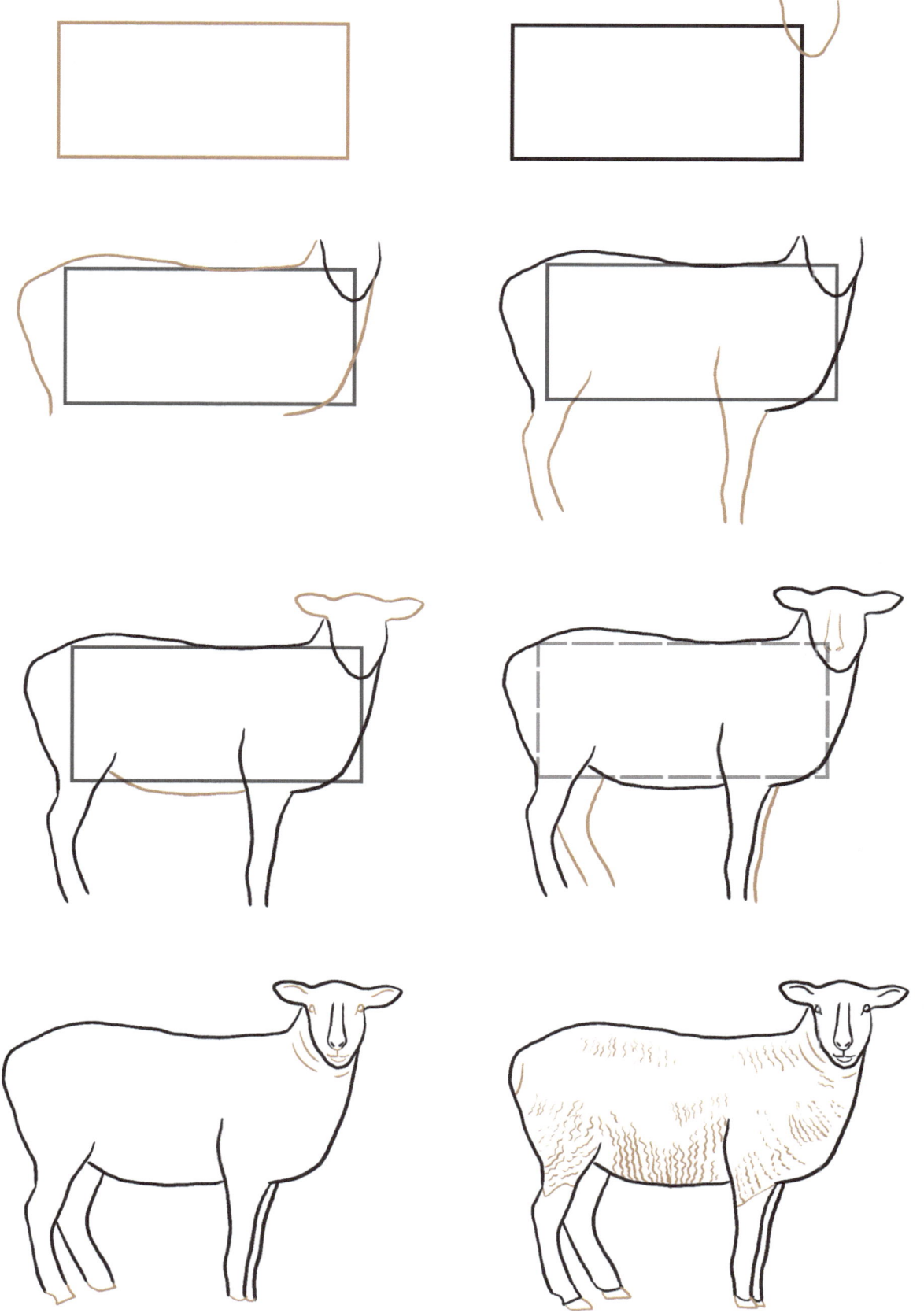

I Heard You Can Draw a...
Ram!

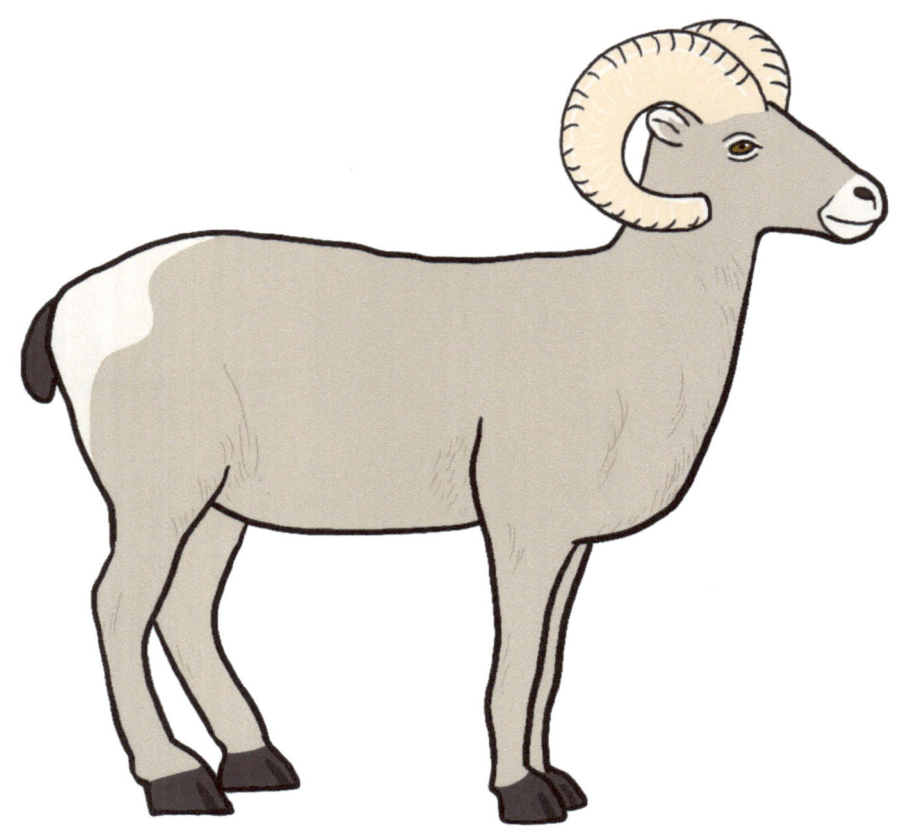

Rams are larger than sheep and have curly horns on their heads.
They are herbivores which means that they eat only plants.

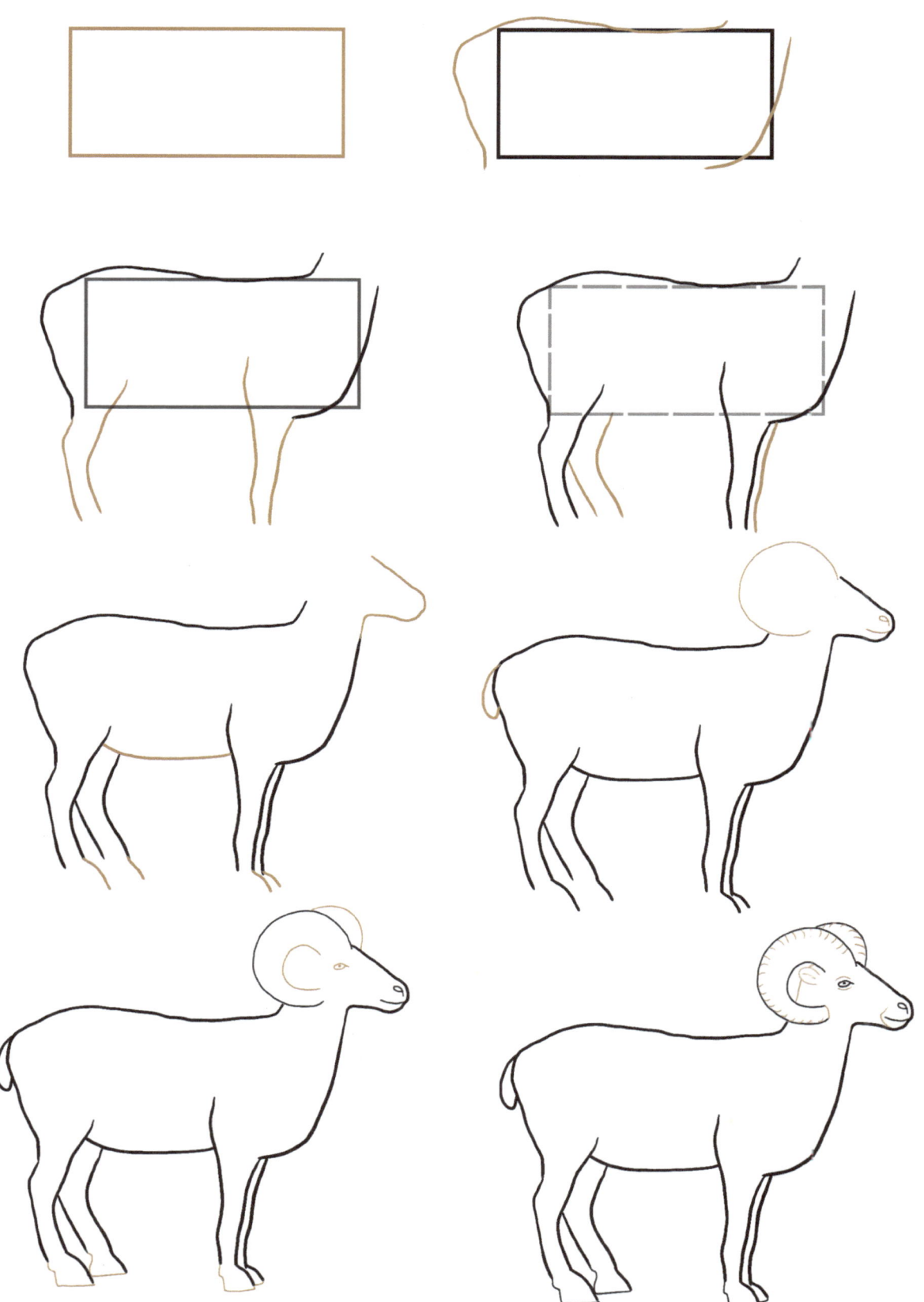

I Heard You Can Draw a...
Goose!

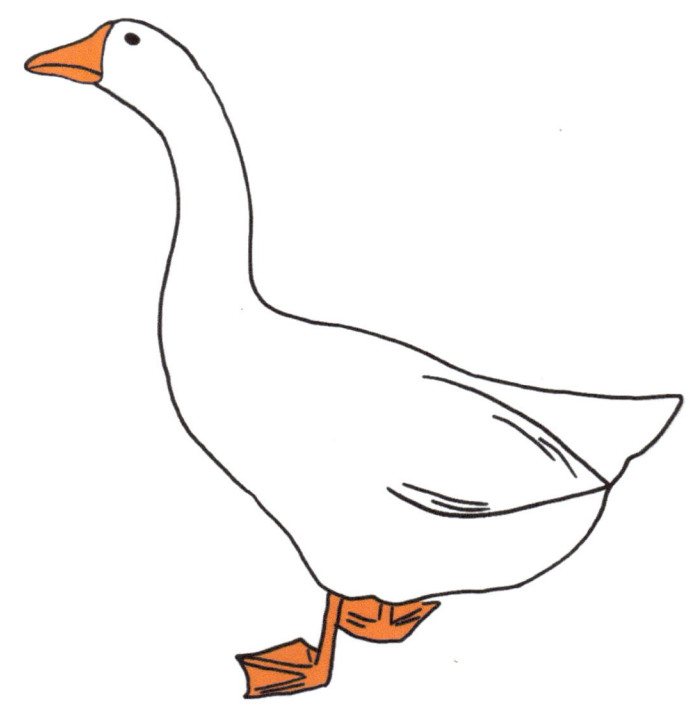

A goose is a waterfowl. They have long necks
and they like to eat grass. A female is called a goose,
a male is called a gander and a baby is called a gosling.

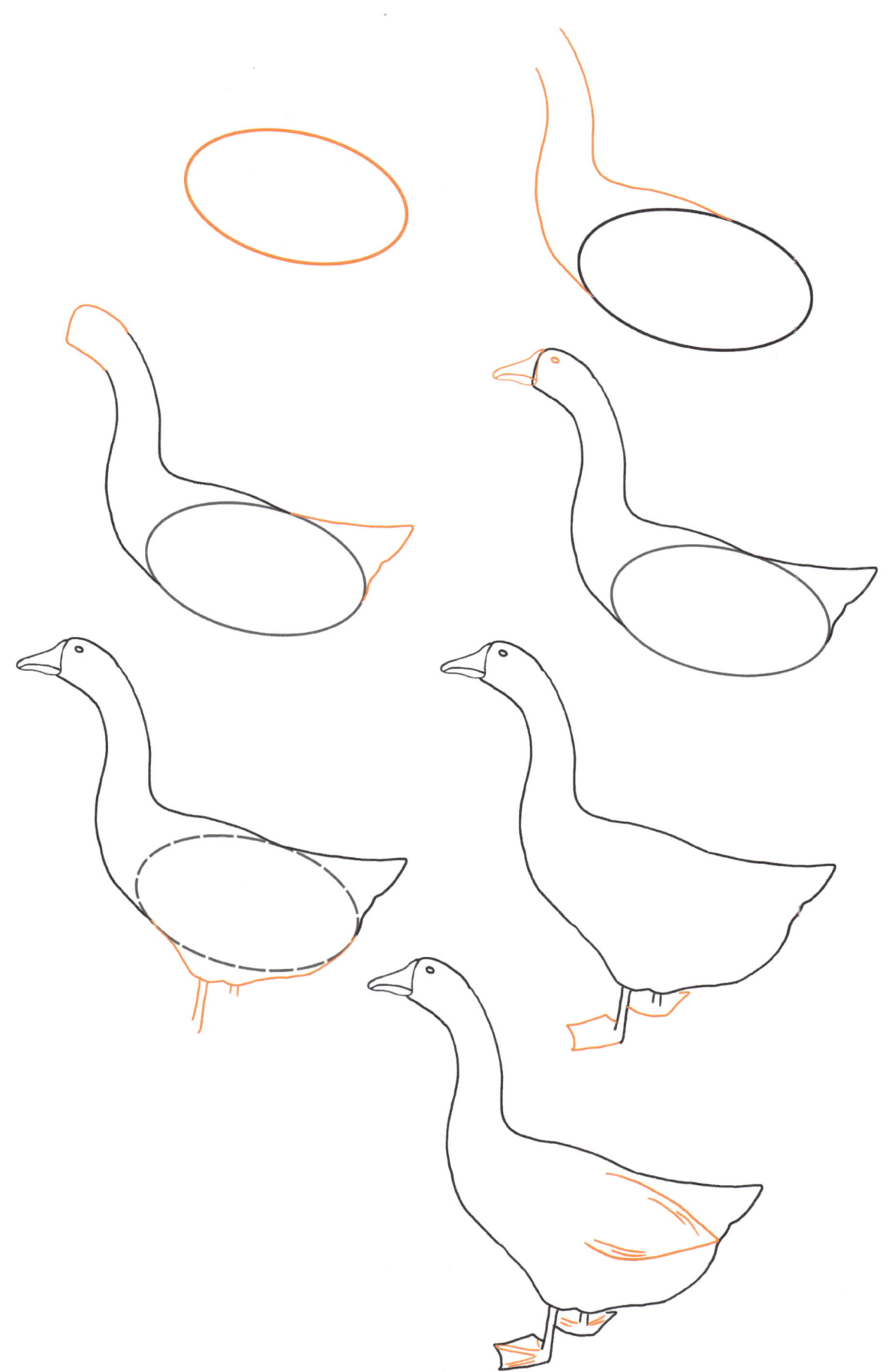

I Heard You Can Draw a...
Pygmy Goat!

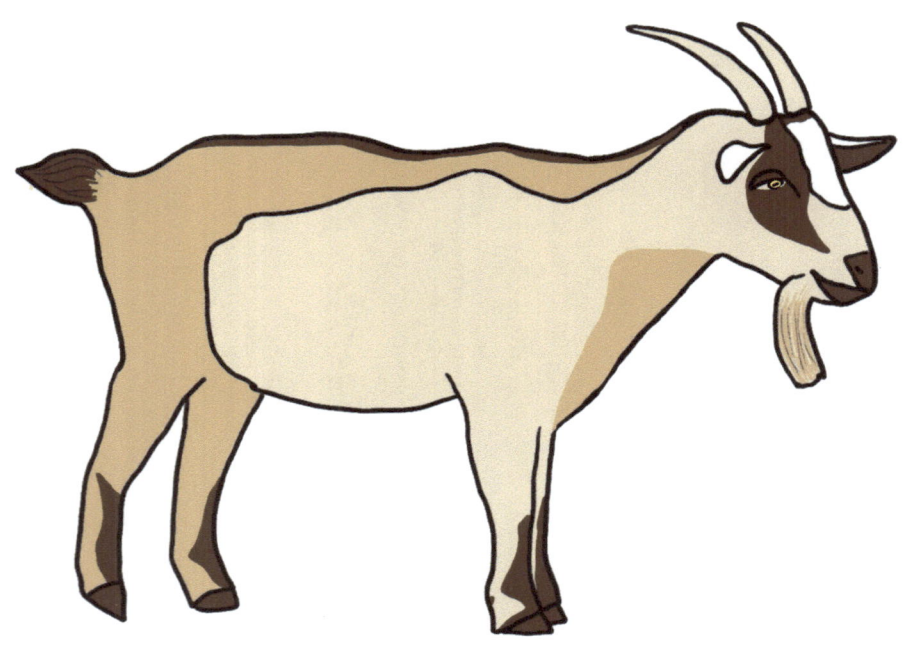

A pygmy goat is a miniature goat. Goats have tails that
stick straight out and beards under their chins!
They like to eat many different plants and they like to climb.
Goats are used on farms to produce milk.

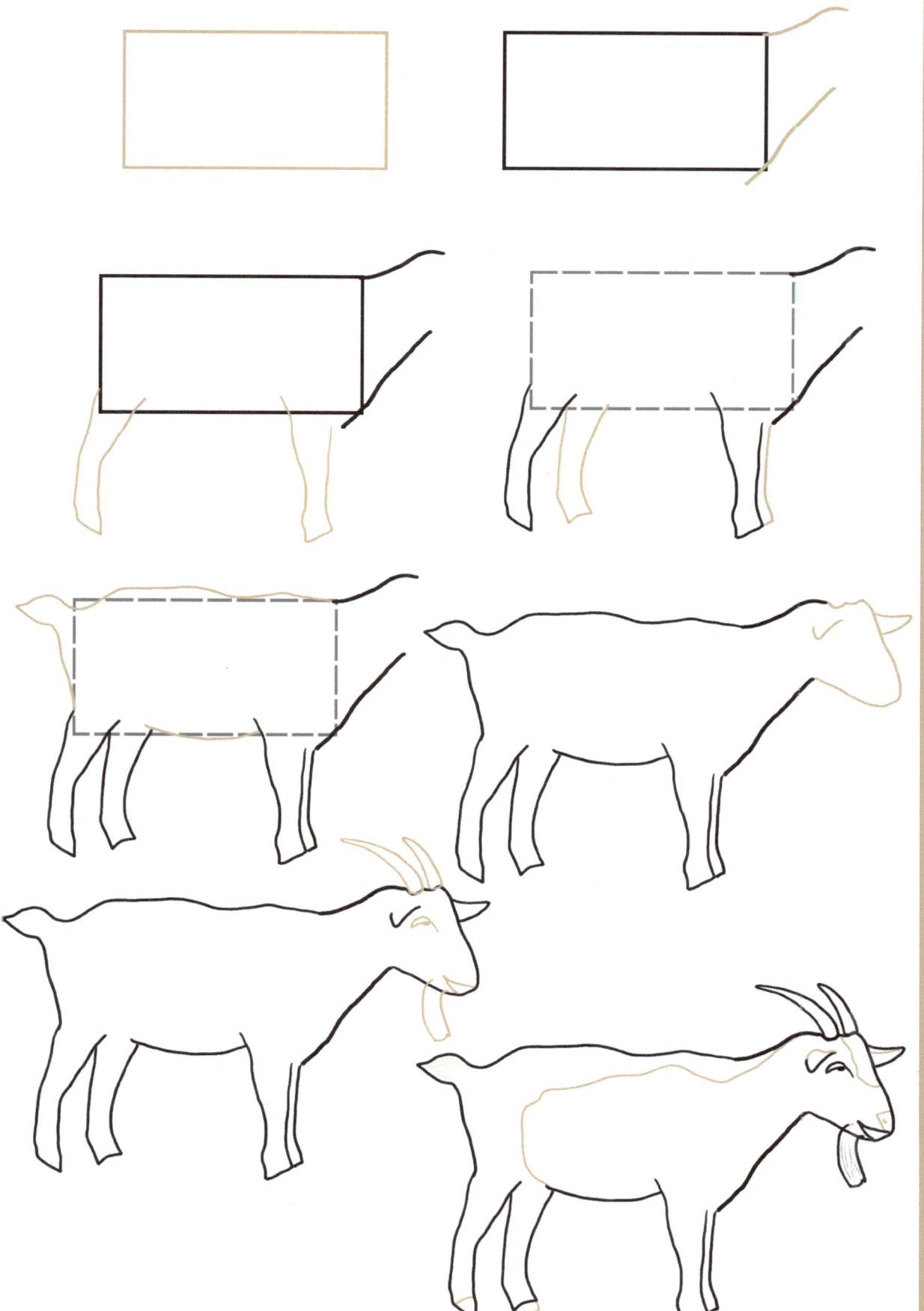

19

I Heard You Can Draw a...
Nubian Goat!

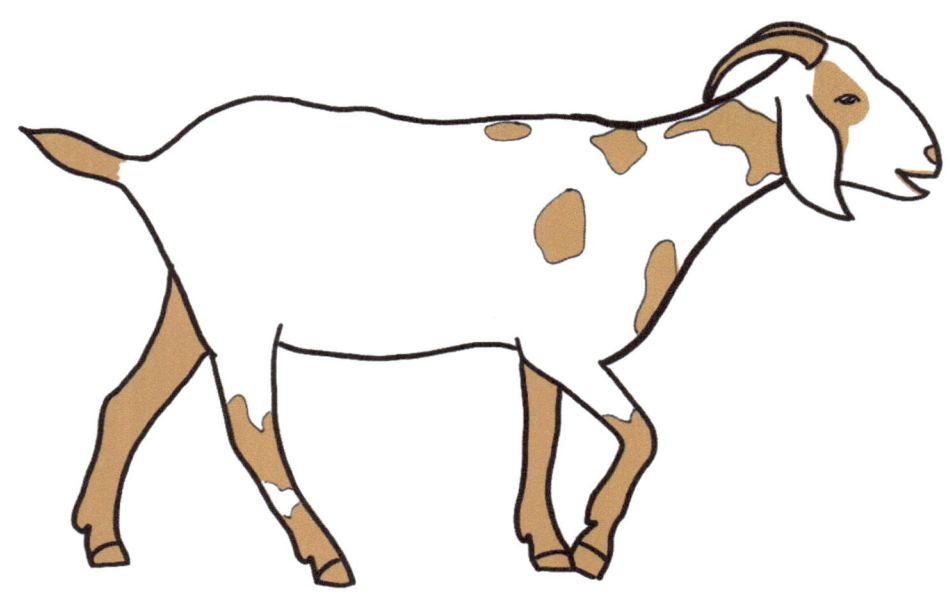

·Nubian goats have long floppy ears and horns on their heads.
Male goats are called bucks, female goats are called does
and the baby goats are called kids. Goats have rectangular
shaped pupils in their eyes which help them see very well.

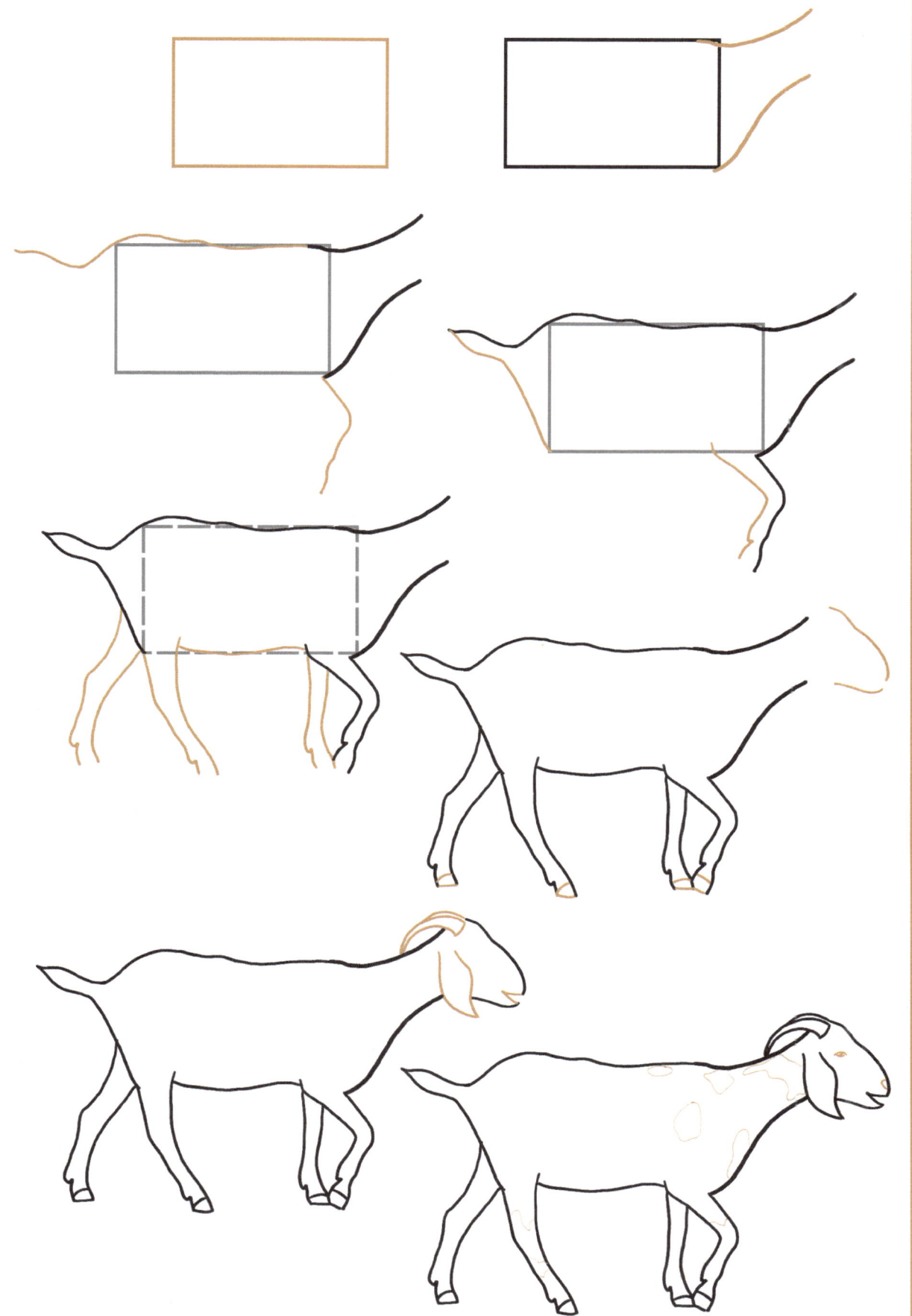

I Heard You Can Draw a...
Mouse!

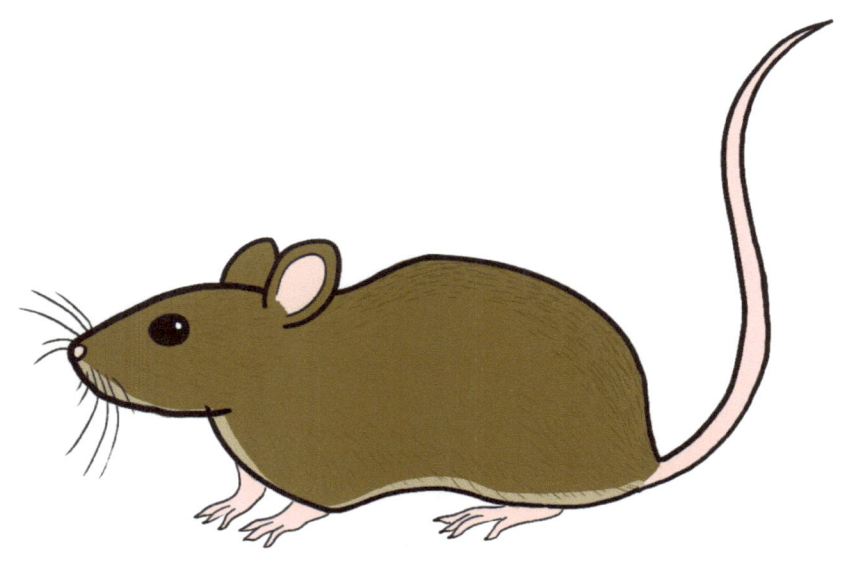

Mice are rodents that have long tails and whiskers.
They are nocturnal which means that they sleep during the day
and they are awake at night.

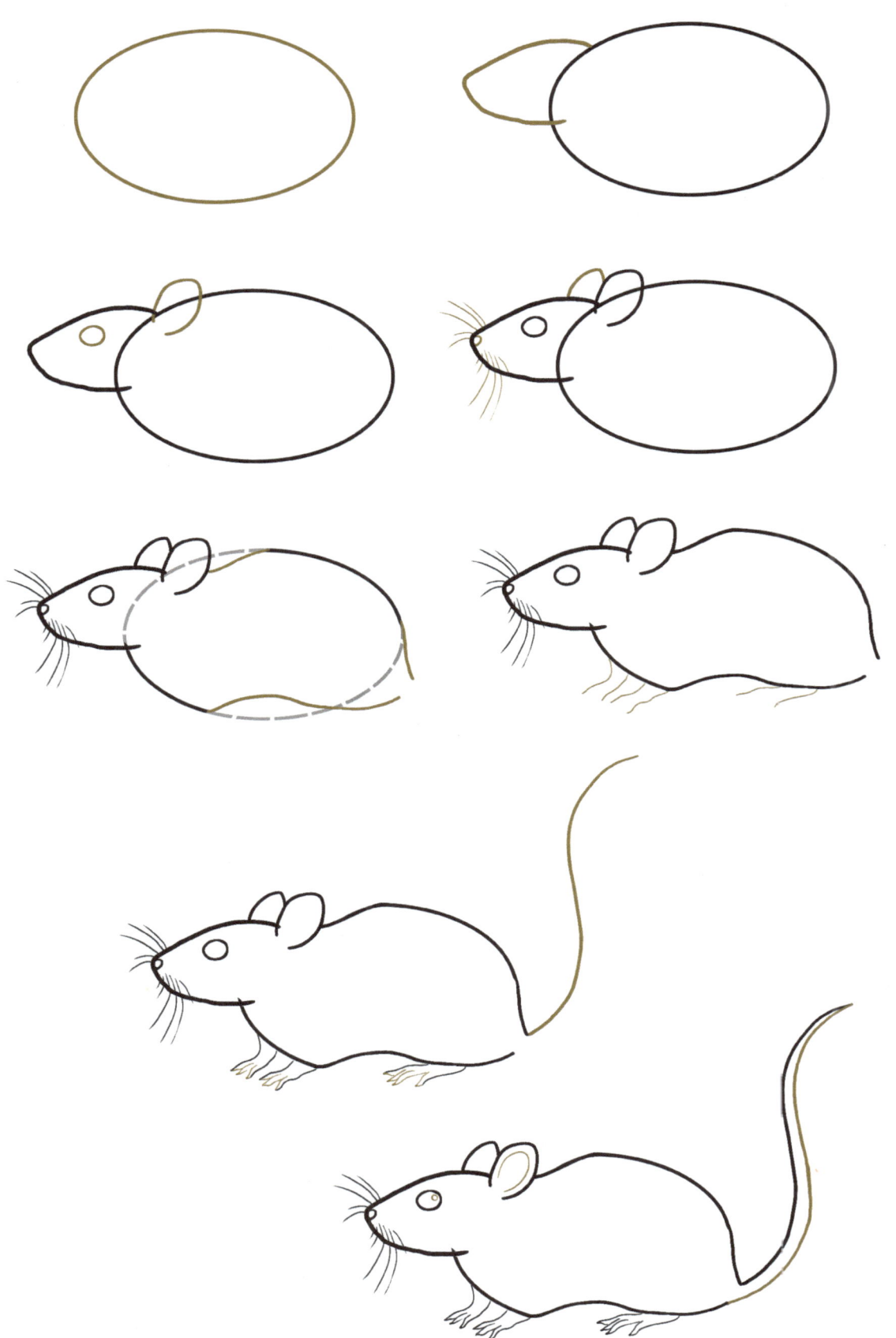

I Heard You Can Draw a...
Squirrel!

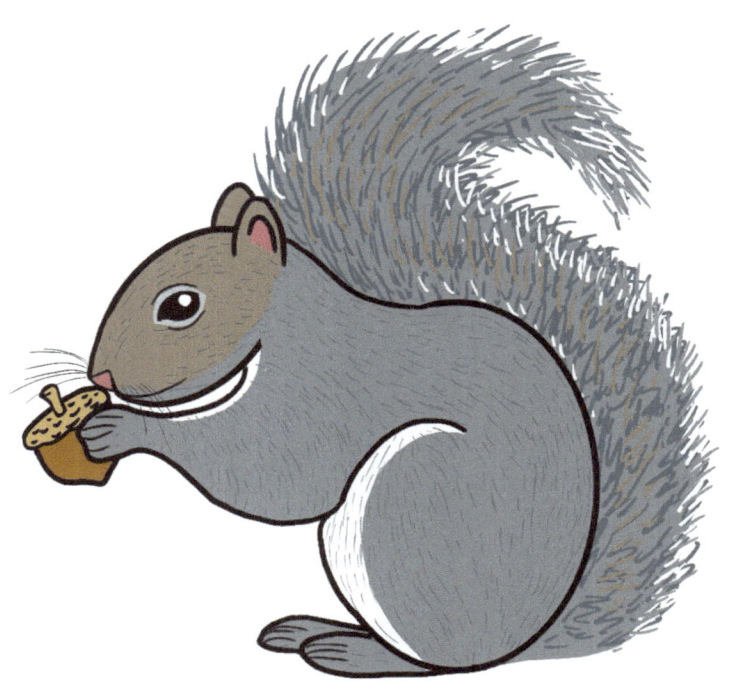

Squirrels are rodents with big bushy tails.
They like to eat nuts, acorns, seeds and more.
Their front teeth never stop growing,
but the food they eat helps to file them down!

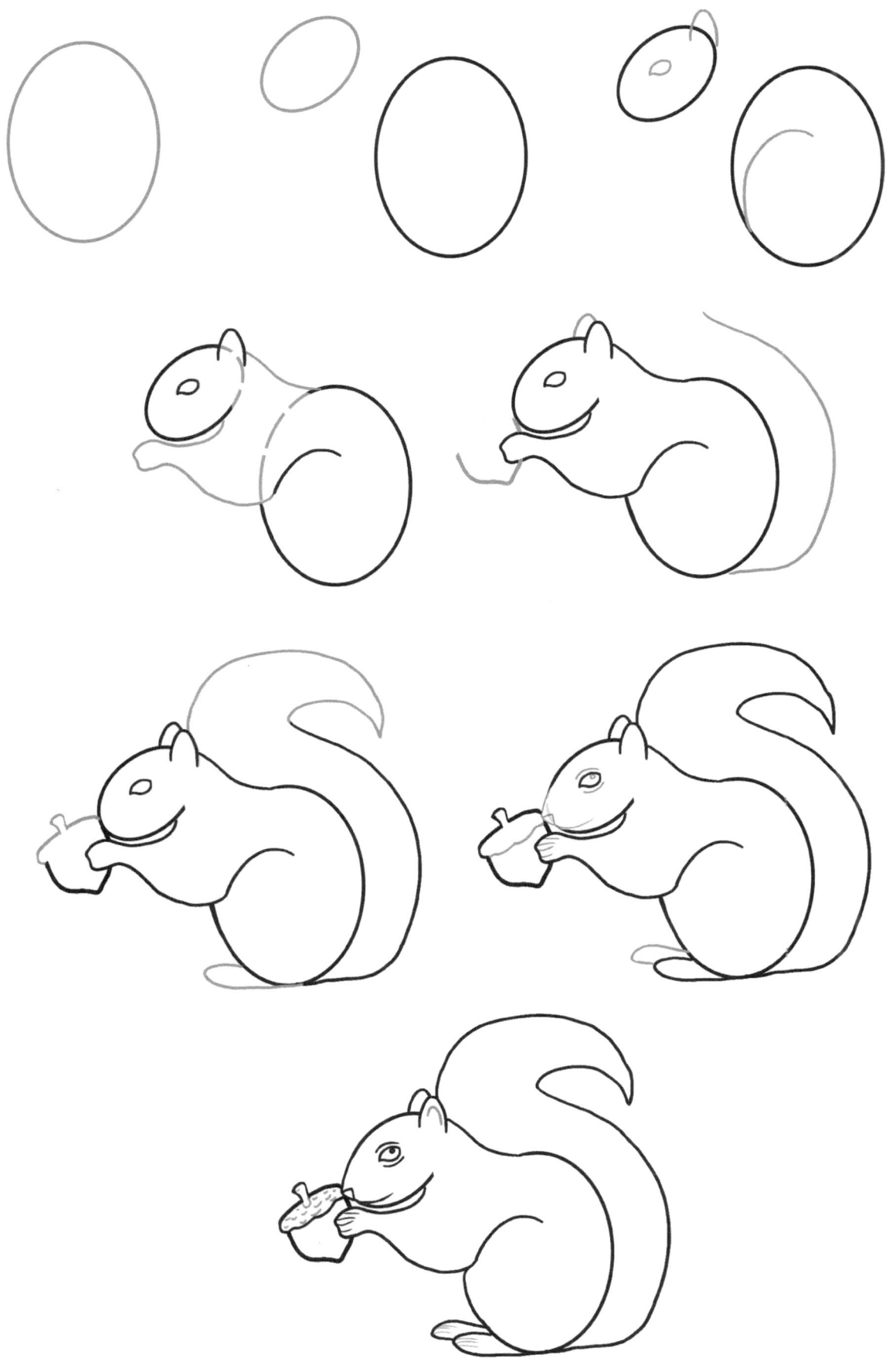

I Heard You Can Draw a...
Cow!

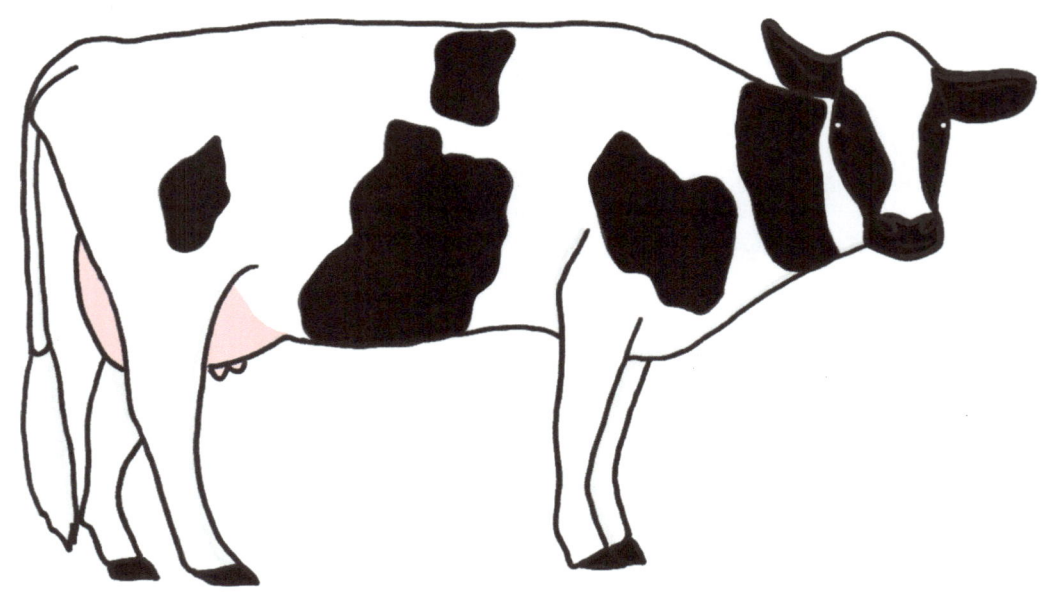

Cows are used on farms to produce milk
and beef. They like to eat grass. Babies are called calves,
males are called bulls and females are called cows.

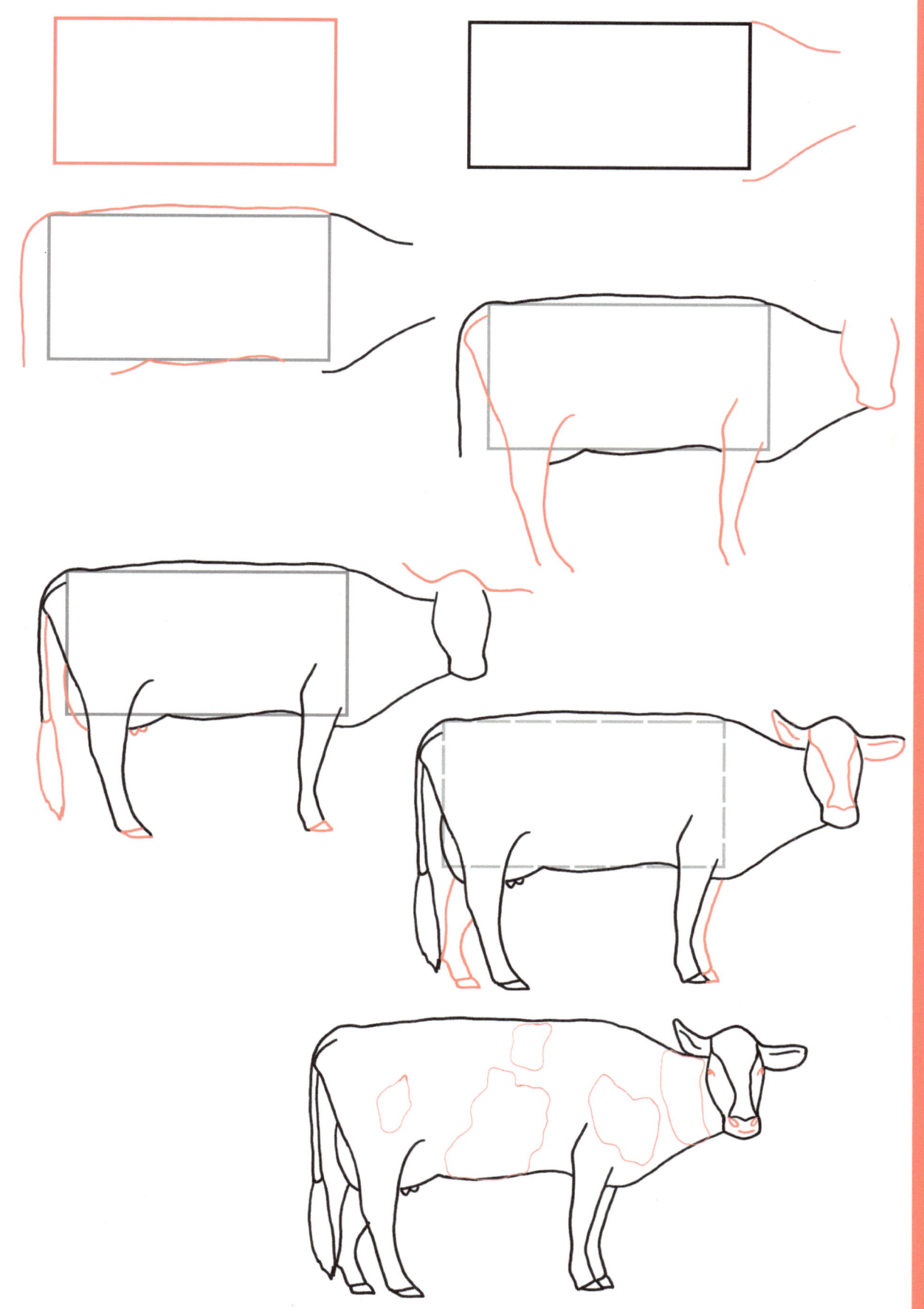

I Heard You Can Draw a...
Bull!

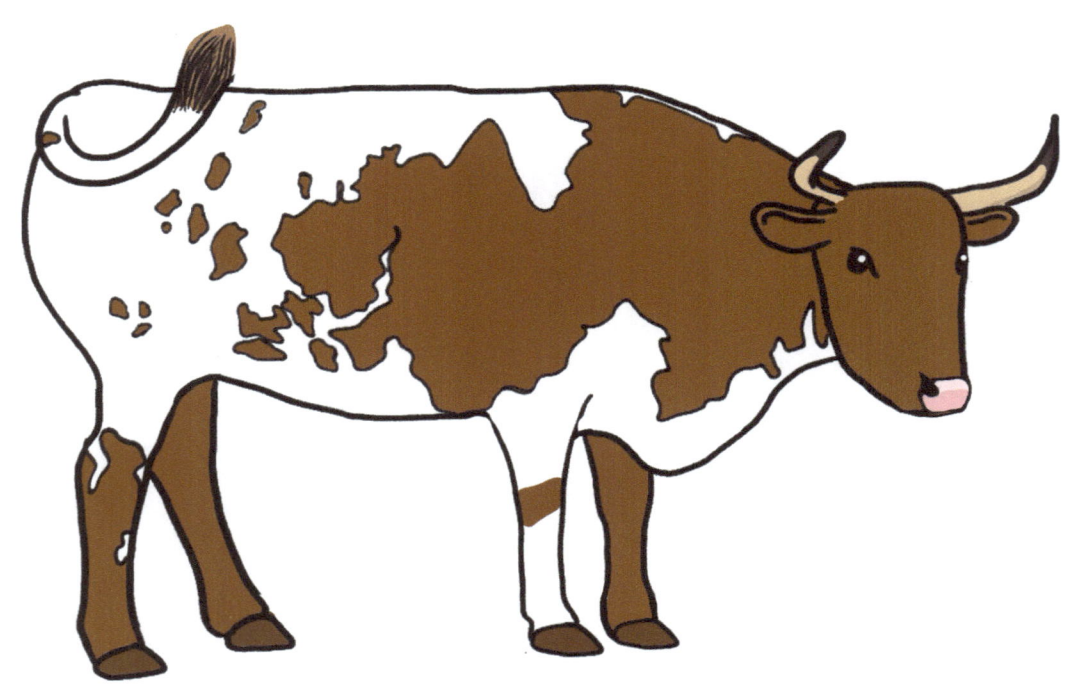

A bull is a male cow.
Bulls are larger than cows and they have horns on their heads.

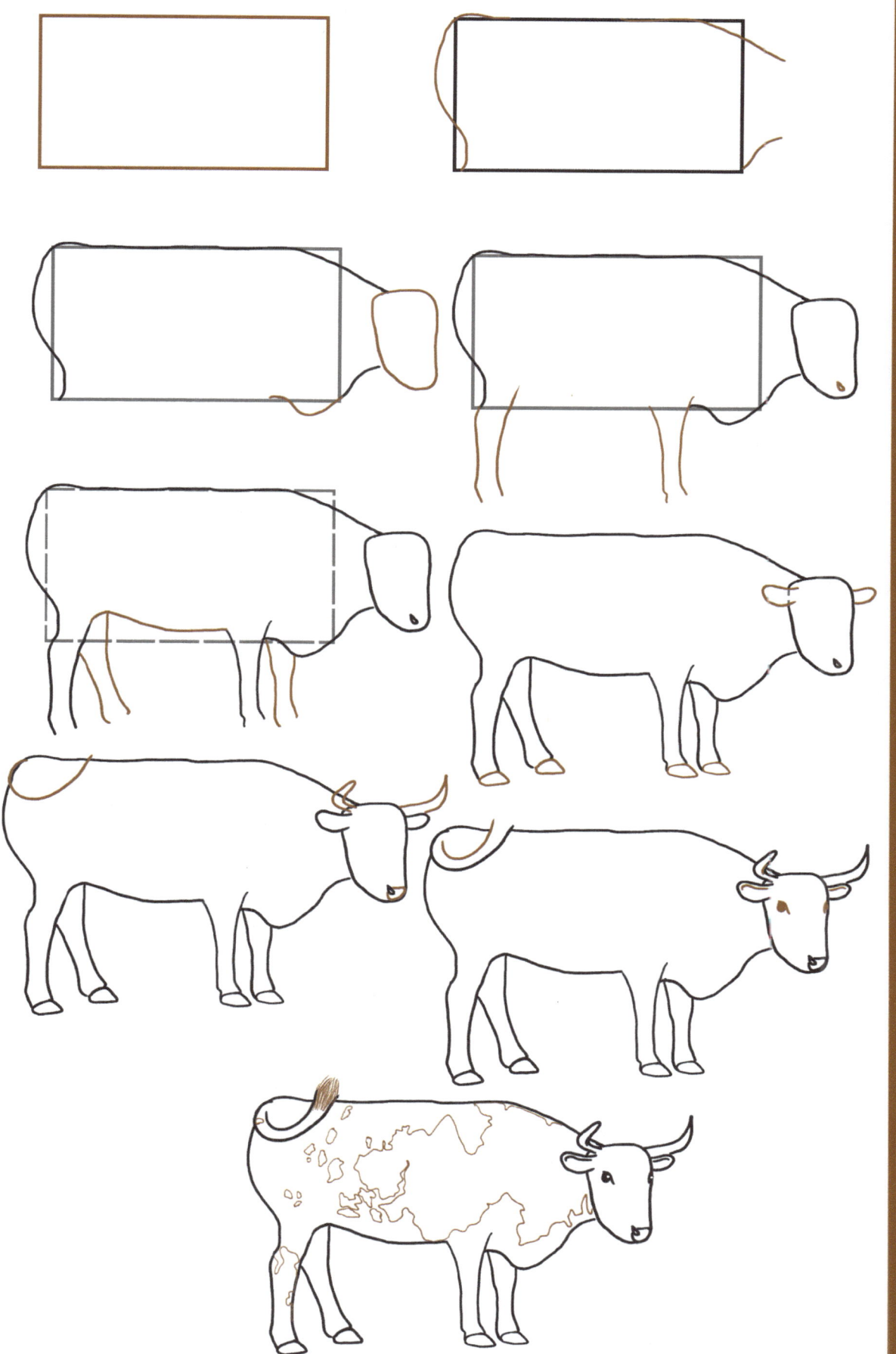

I Heard You Can Draw a...
Crow!

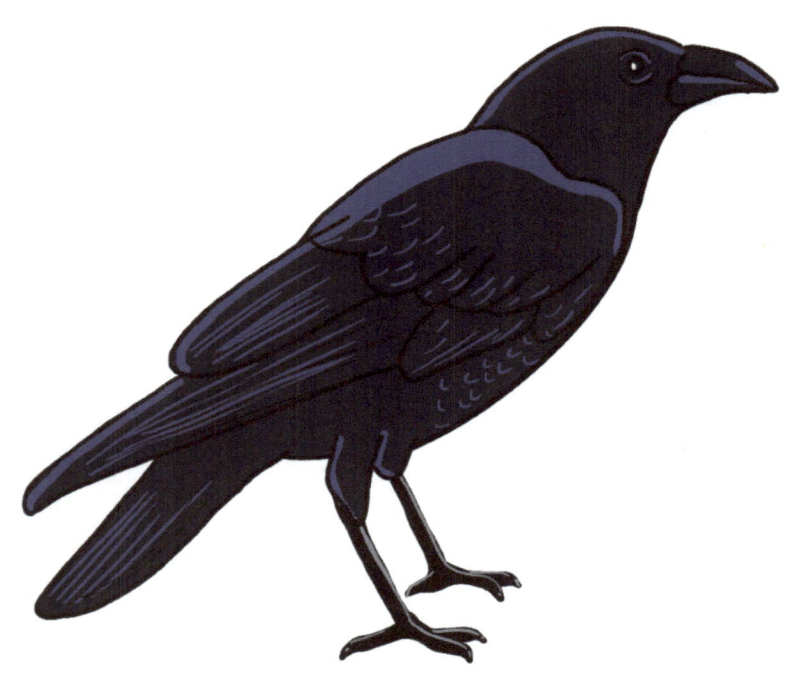

Crows are black birds. They are omnivores
which means that they eat both plants and animals.

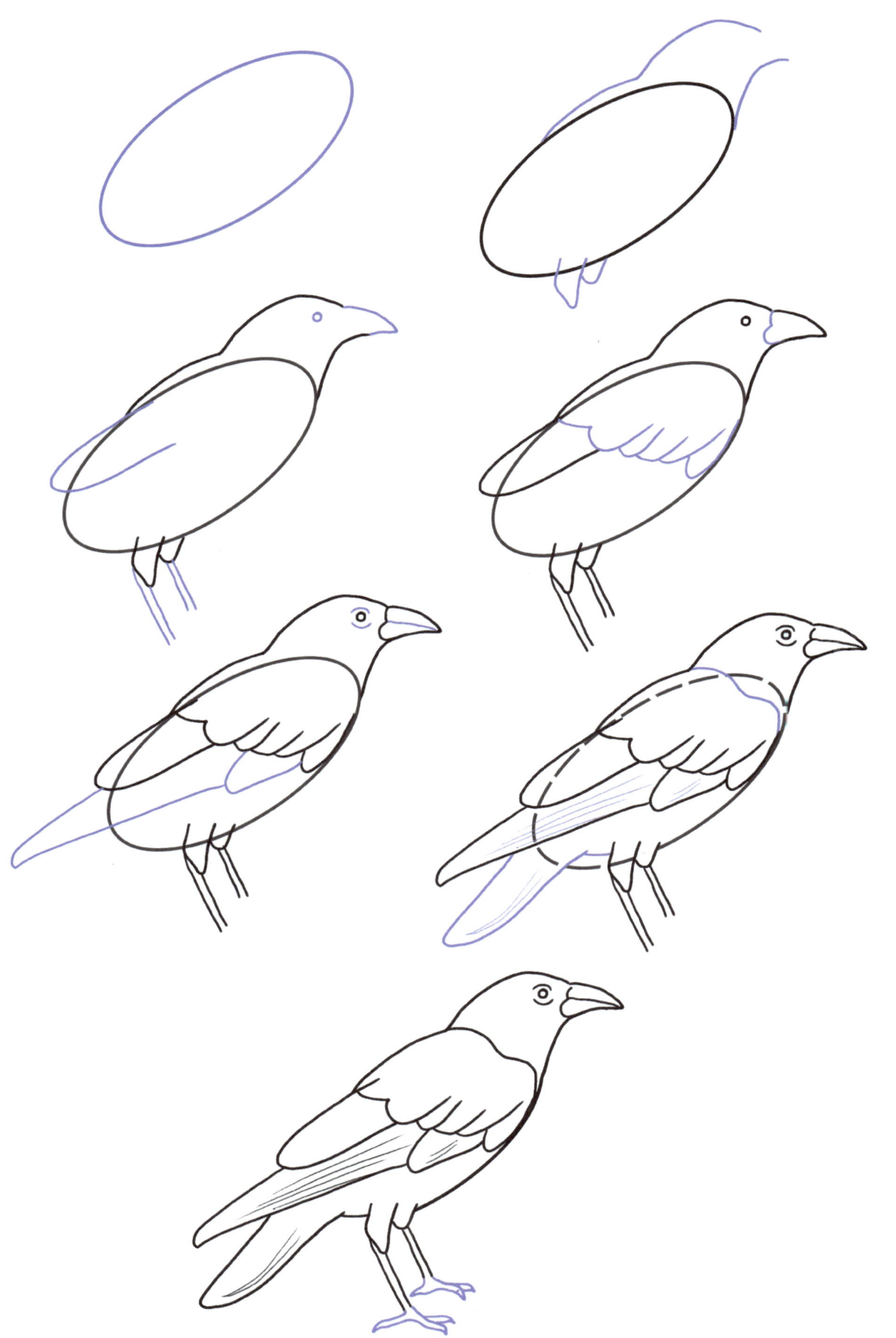

I Heard You Can Draw a...
Dragonfly!

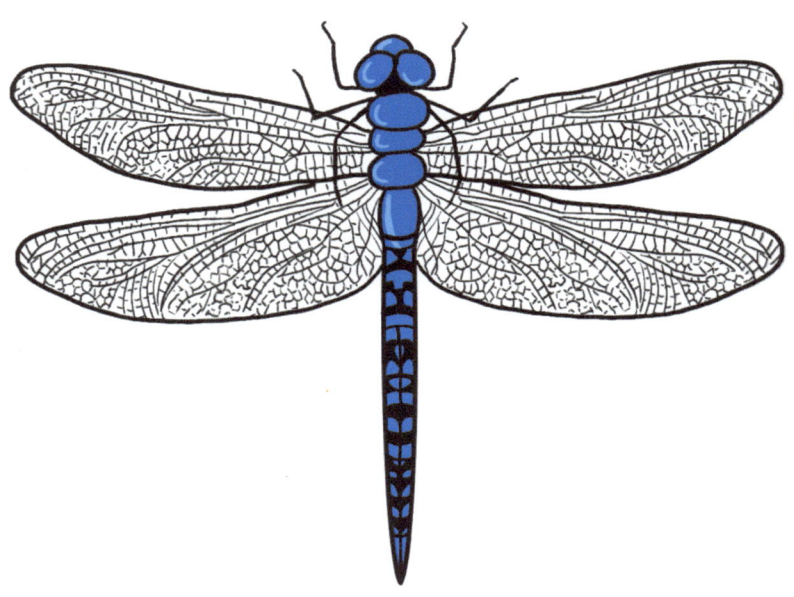

Dragonflies have been around for millions of years!
They eat other insects, like mosquitoes. Each dragonfly has six legs
and two pairs of wings which makes them very fast fliers.
Dragonflies do not sting or bite people.

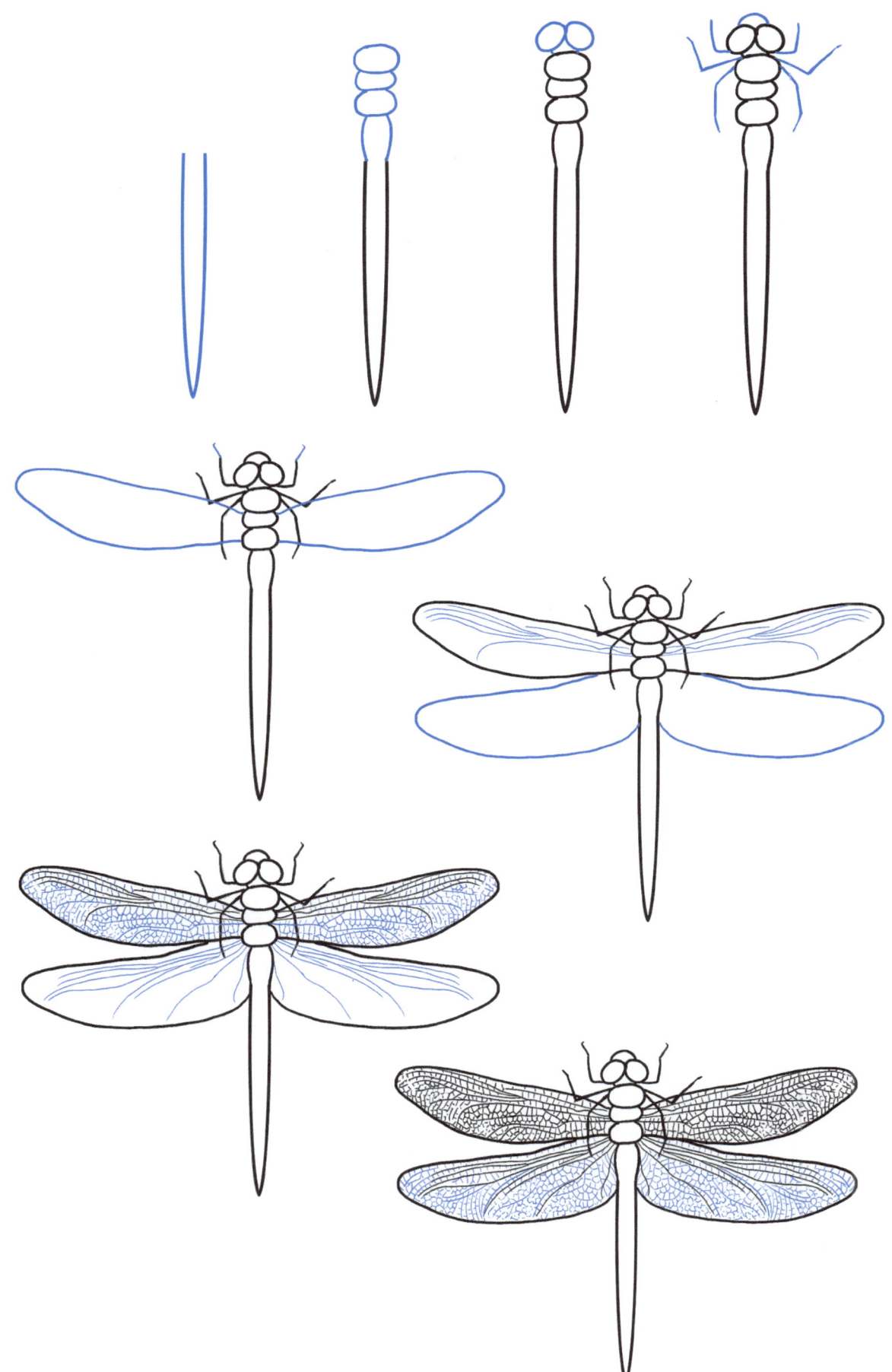

I Heard You Can Draw a...
Donkey!

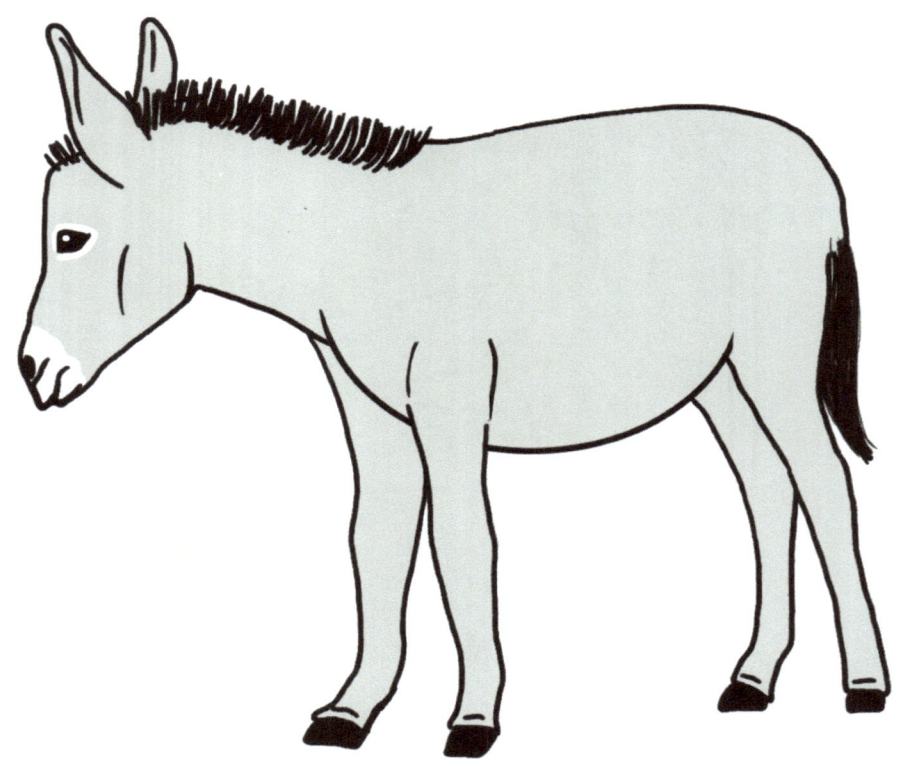

Donkeys are from the Middle East and Africa.
They have long ears and they are related to horses.
Donkeys protect the farm animals from predators,
like foxes and coyotes, by chasing them away.

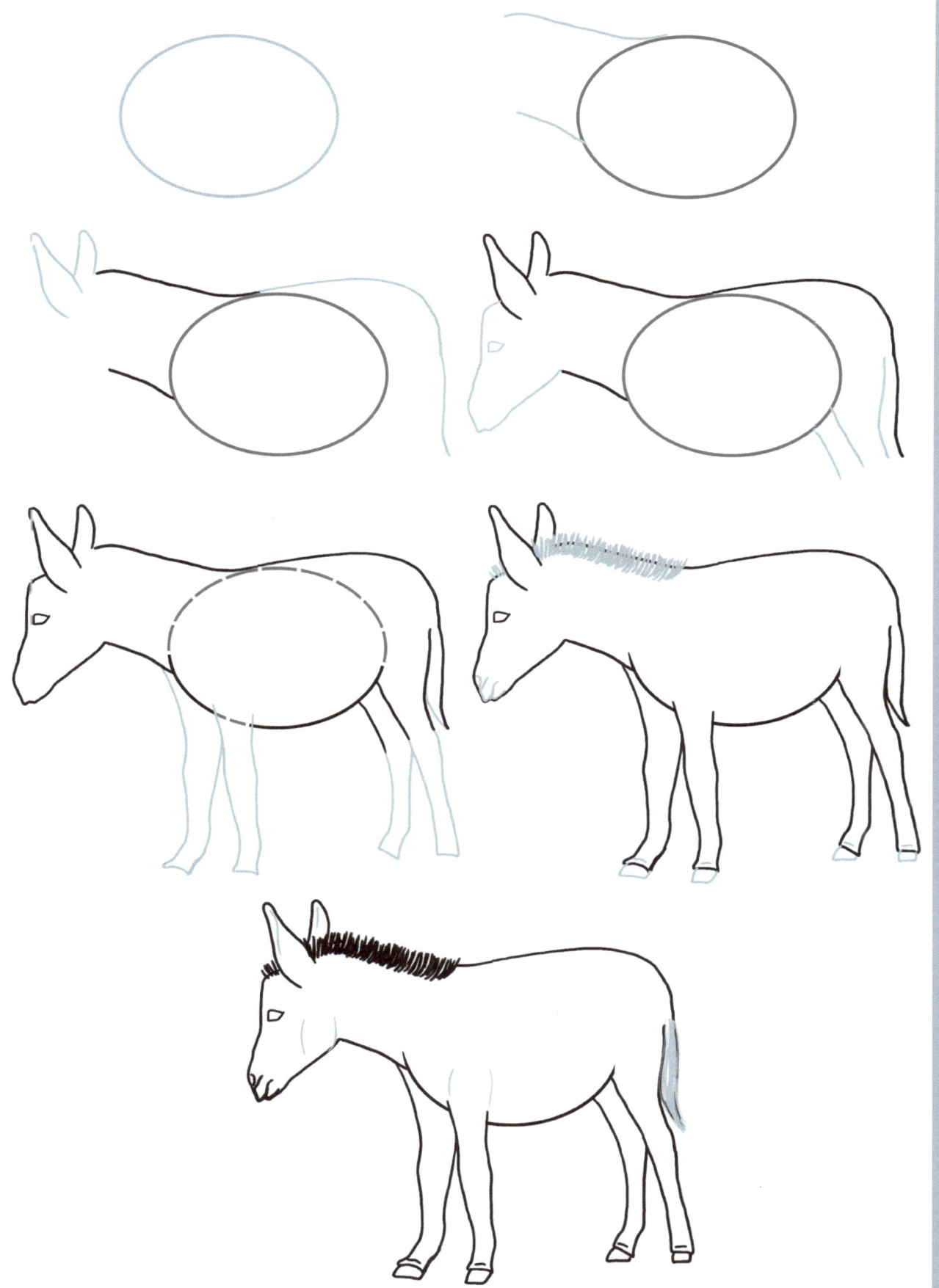

I Heard You Can Draw a...
Pig!

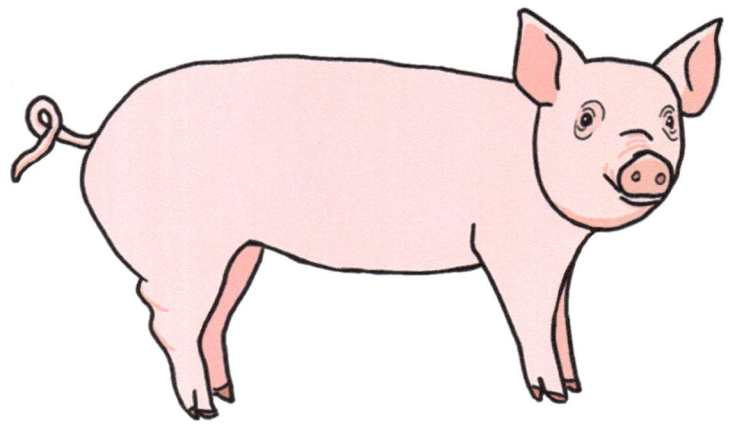

Pigs have noses that are called snouts.
Male pigs are called boars and females are called sows.
Their babies are called piglets.

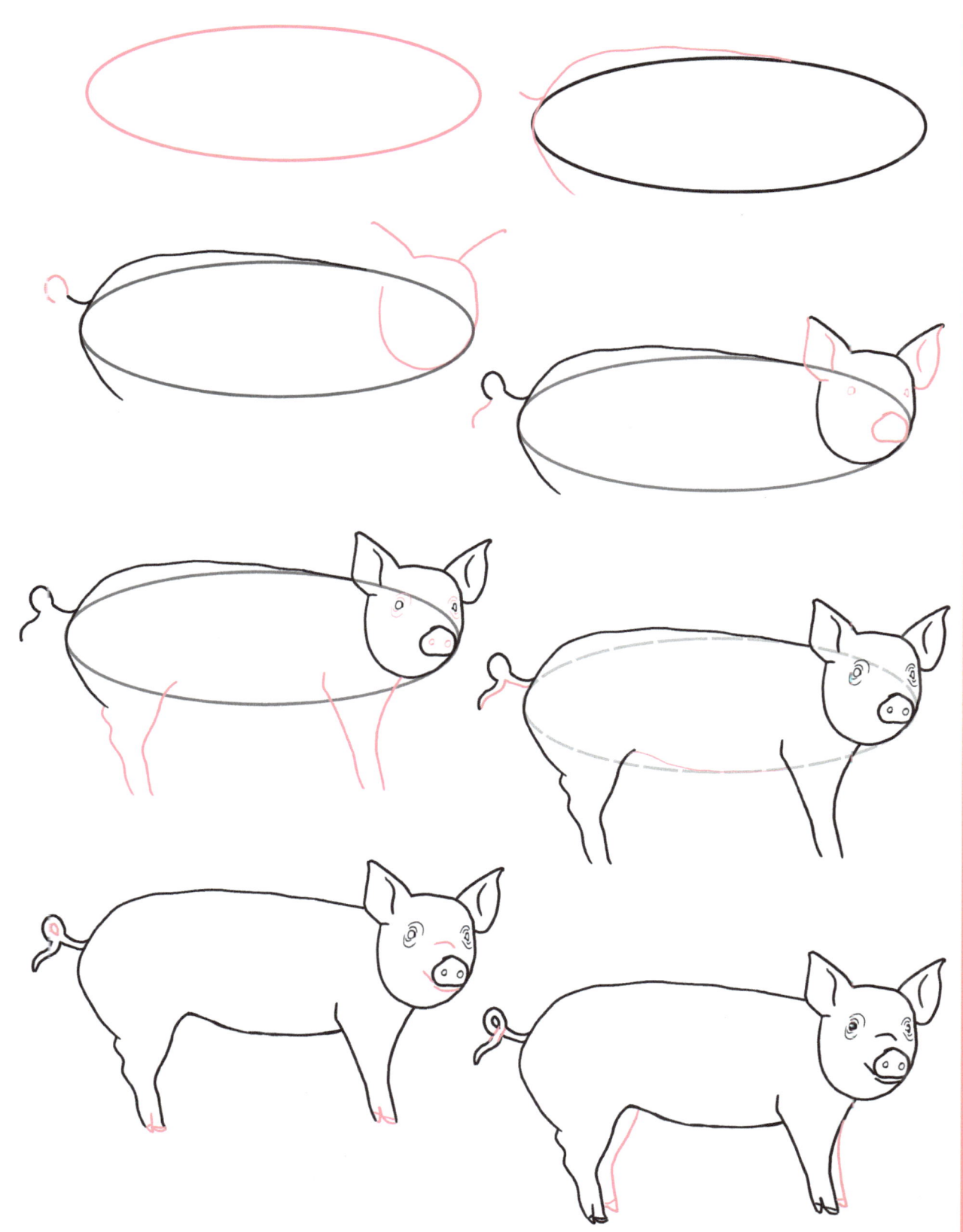

37

I Heard You Can Draw a...
Scarecrow!

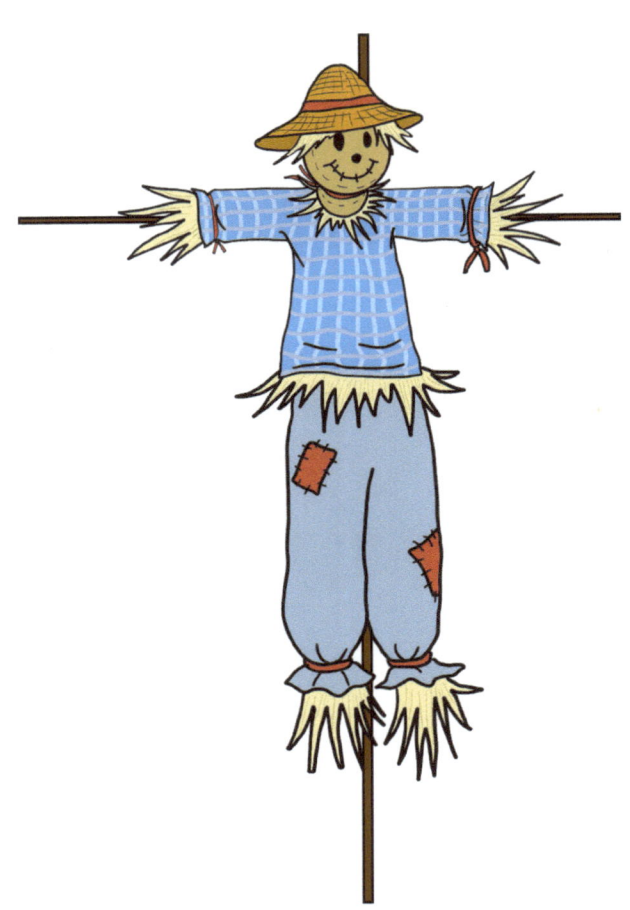

A scarecrow is made in the shape of a human with old clothes stuffed with hay. Farmers place them in their fields to scare away crows and other animals that could eat their crops. Scarecrows have been around for hundreds of years!

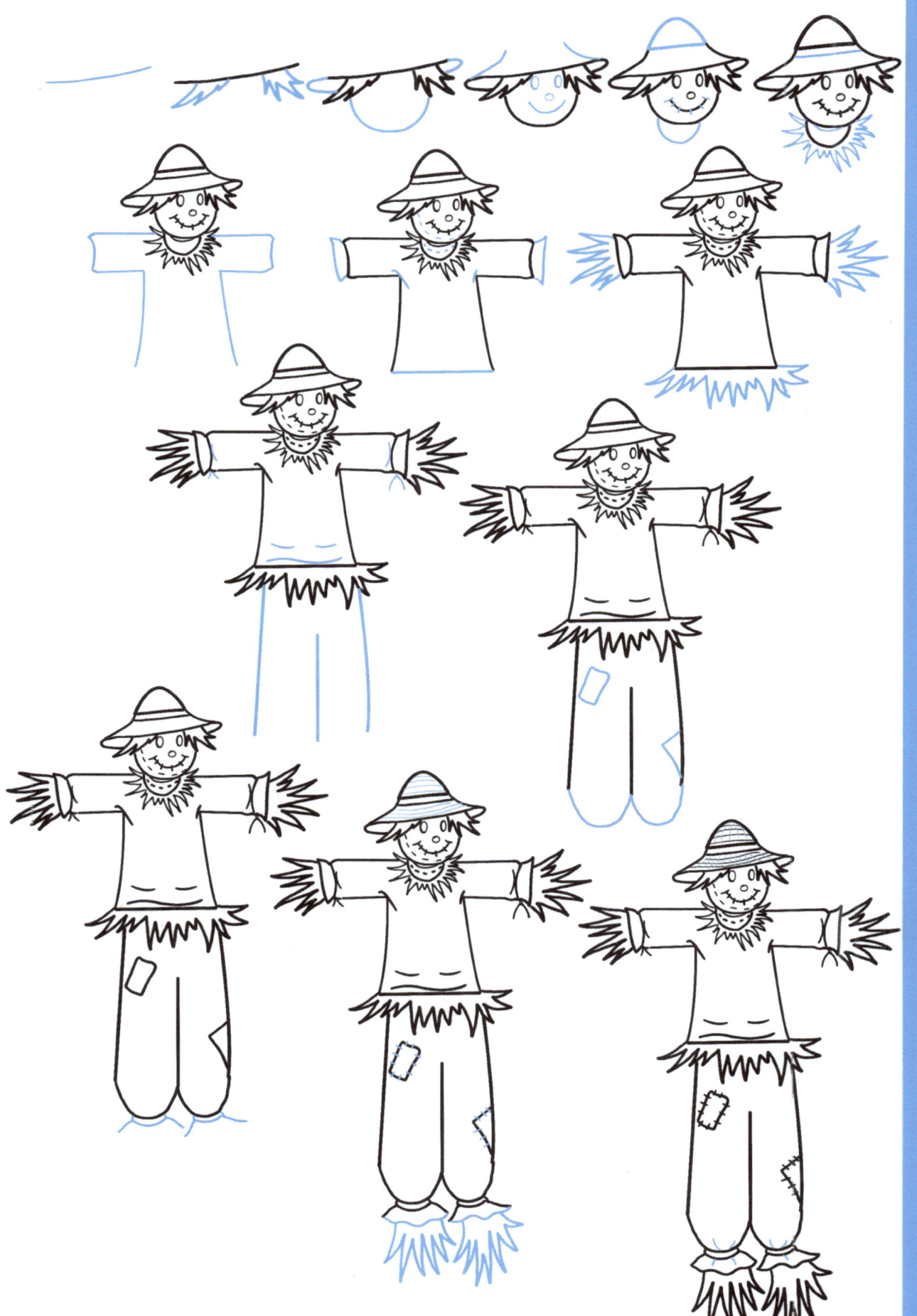

I Heard You Can Draw a...
Barn!

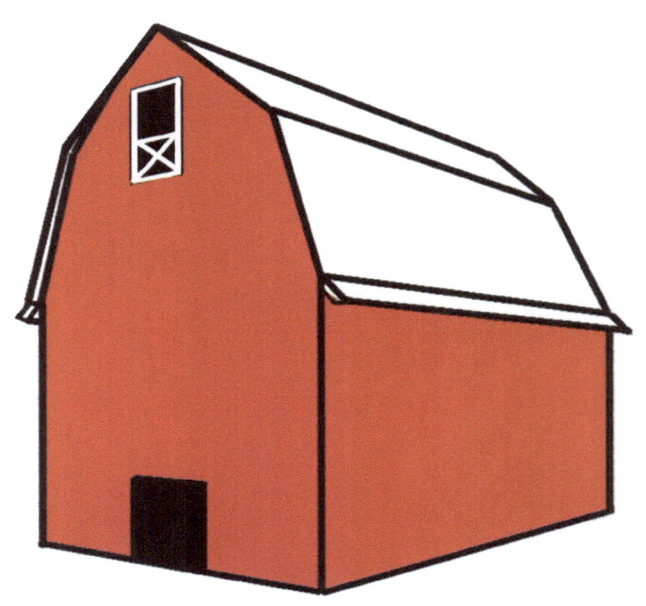

A barn is a building where farm animals live and where food is stored.
We are going to draw the barn using **two-point perspective**.
Two-point perspective is when something is viewed from
the corner and both sides seem to get smaller in size
as they move toward two vanishing points.

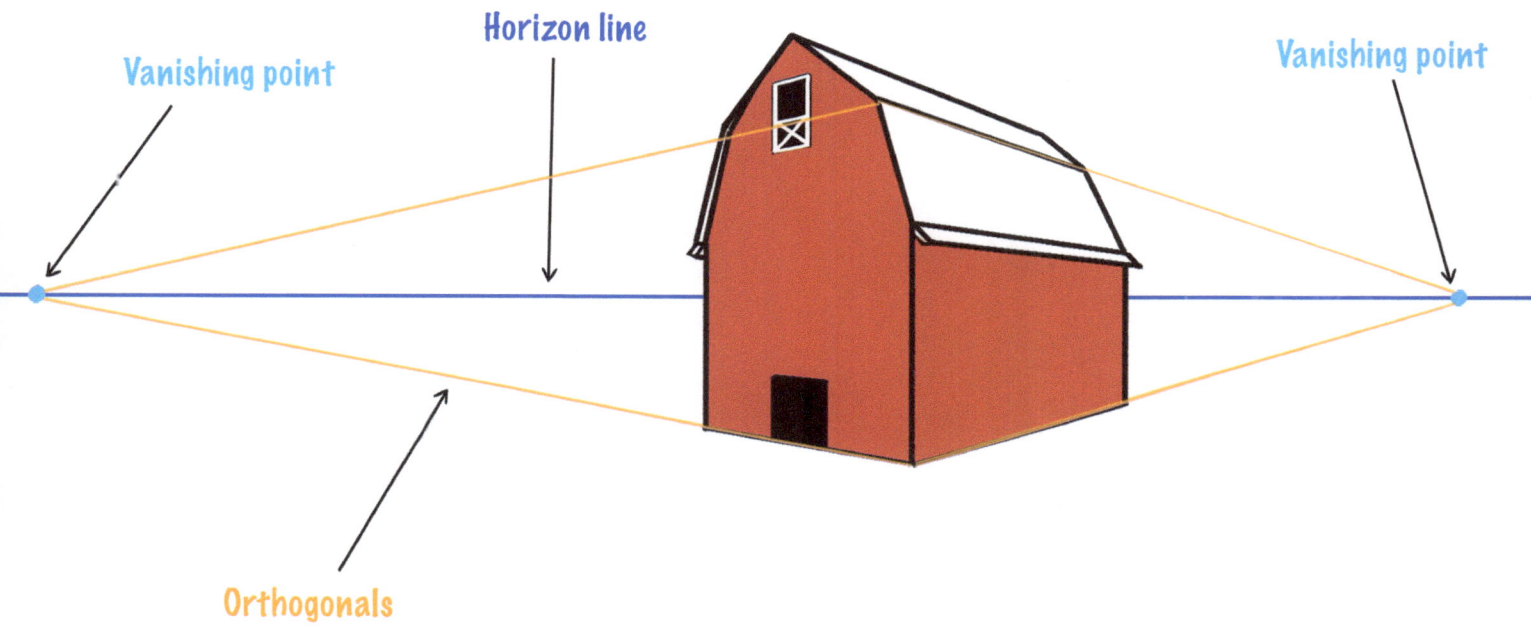

Vanishing point

Horizon line

Vanishing point

Orthogonals

Vanishing point = an invisible point where it seems like an object's lines would meet if they extended that far. In two-point perspective, there are two vanishing points.

Horizon line = The "line" that forms in the distance where it looks like the sky touches the ground.

Orthogonals = Diagonal lines that are used to find angles in two-point perspective drawings. They are invisible lines that go from the building's corners to the vanishing points.

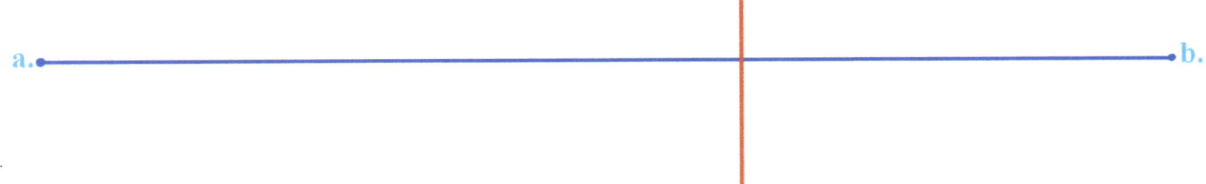

1. Draw a horizontal line. This is the **horizon line**. The dots at each end are the **vanishing points**.

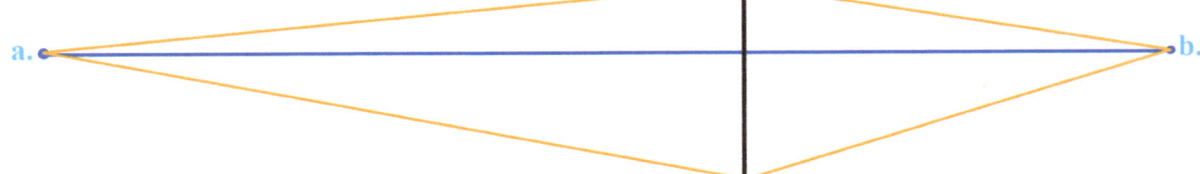

2. Draw a vertical line that crosses through the horizon line. This will be the corner of the barn.

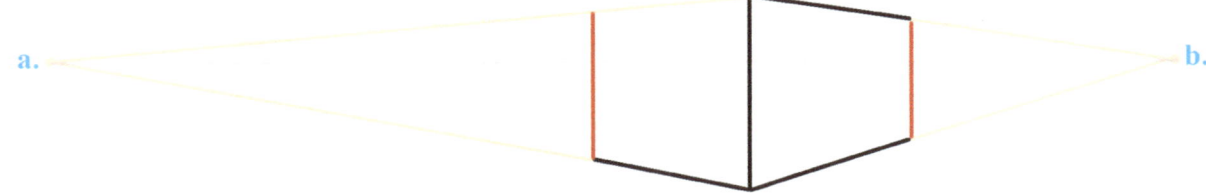

3. Draw **orthogonal** lines from each end of the vertical line to vanishing points **a** and **b**.

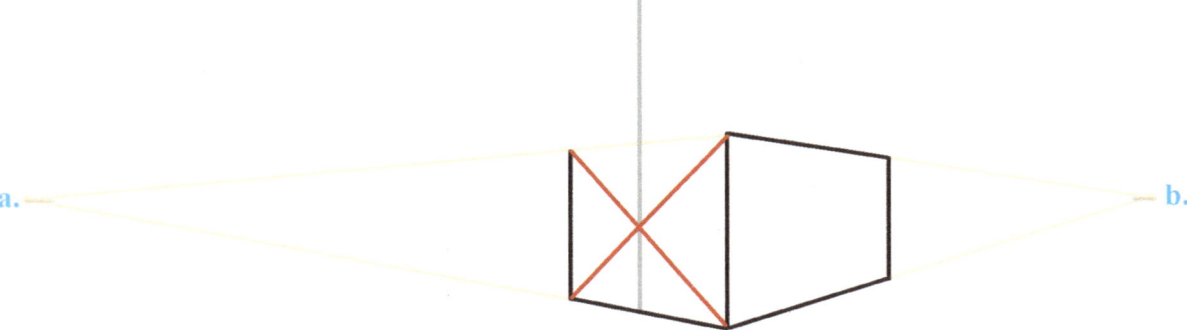

4. Decide how wide each side of the barn will be and draw two vertical lines to show the sides.

5. Find the center of the left side by drawing an X. The middle of the X is the middle of that side.

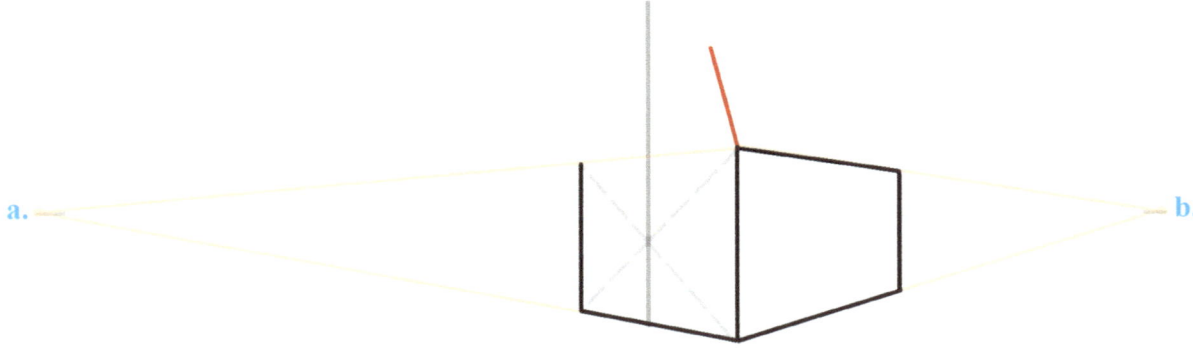

6. Draw a slanted line from the top of the corner.

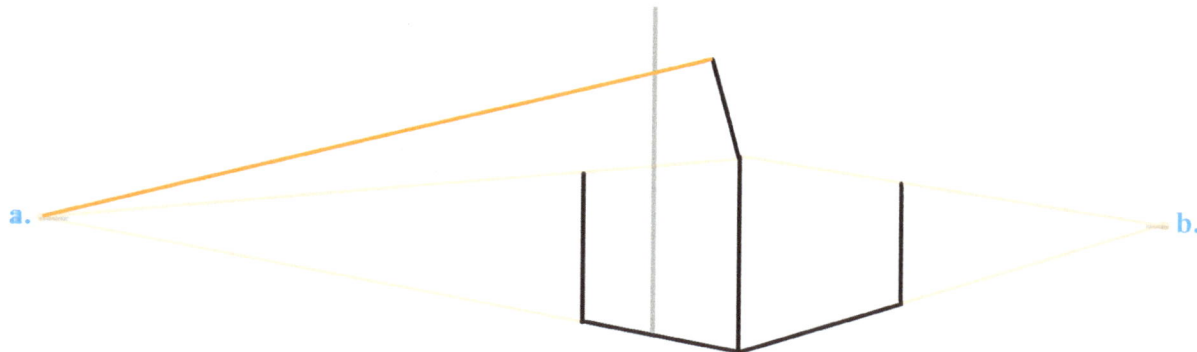

7. From the top of the line, draw an **orthogonal** line that touches vanishing point **a**.

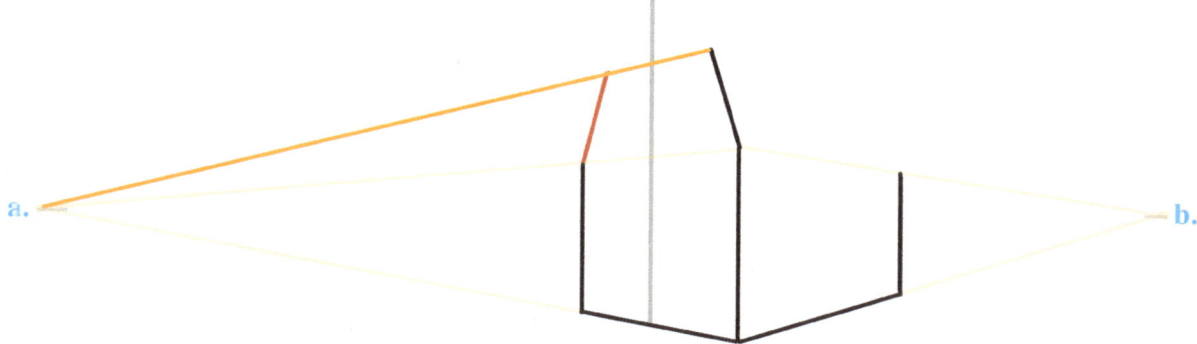

8. Draw a slanted line from the left side of the barn to the top of the **orthogonal**.

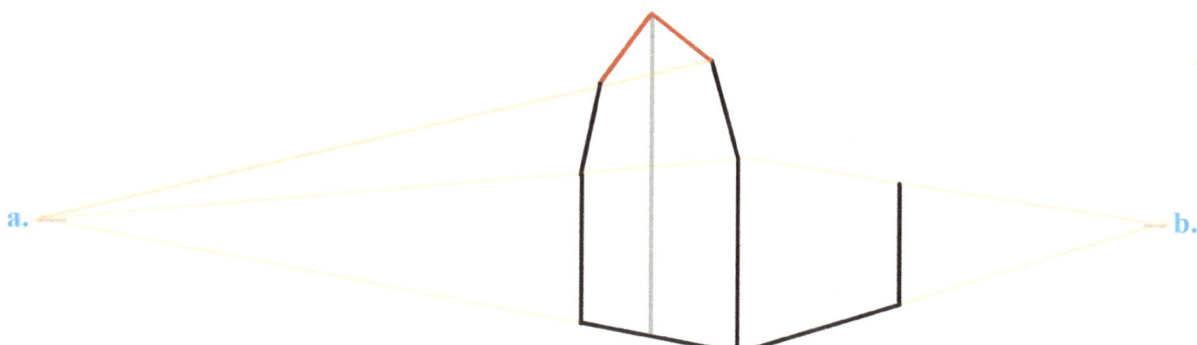

9. Draw two slanted lines that meet at the center line.

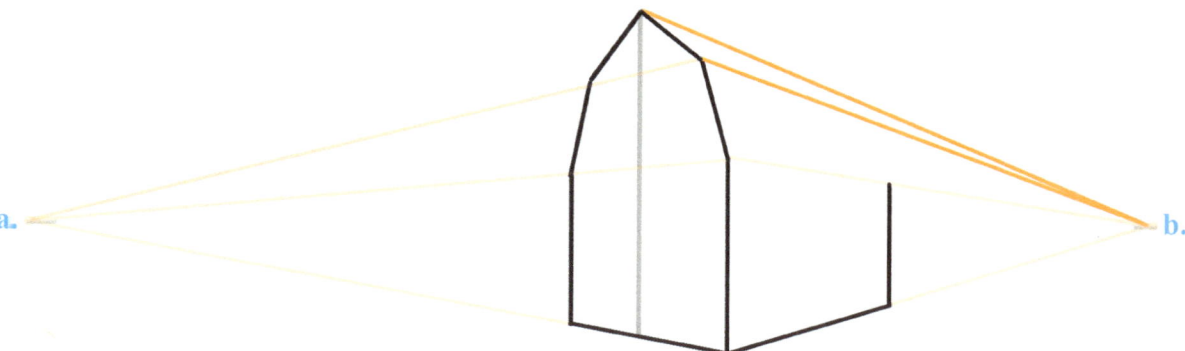

10. Draw two **orthogonal** lines starting from the top points to vanishing point **b**.

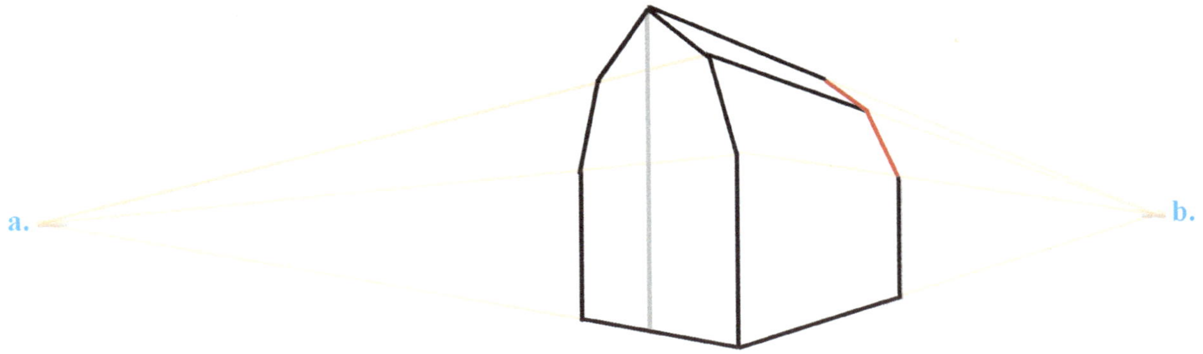

11. Add the back of the roof.

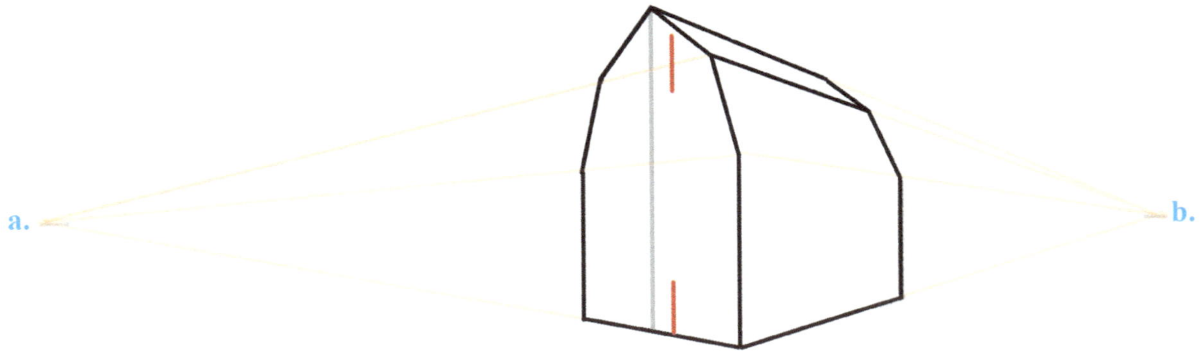

12. Draw two vertical lines, one for the opening at the top and one for the door.

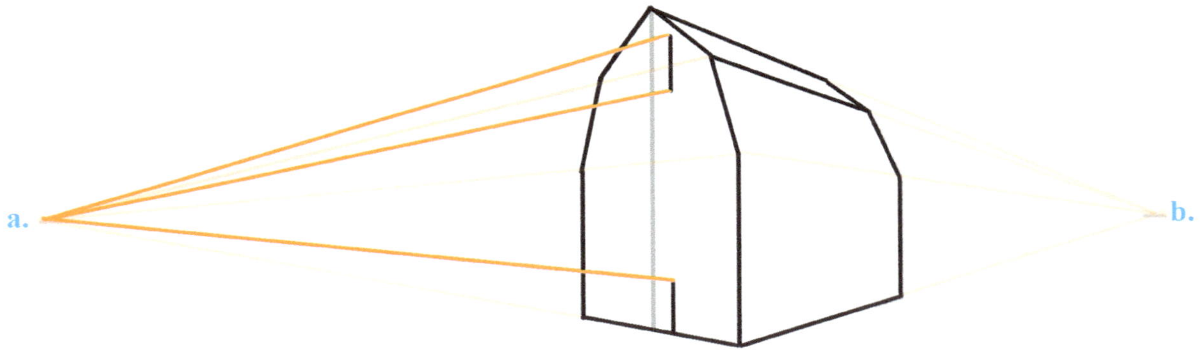

13. Draw 3 orthogonal lines from the end of the vertical lines to vanishing point a.

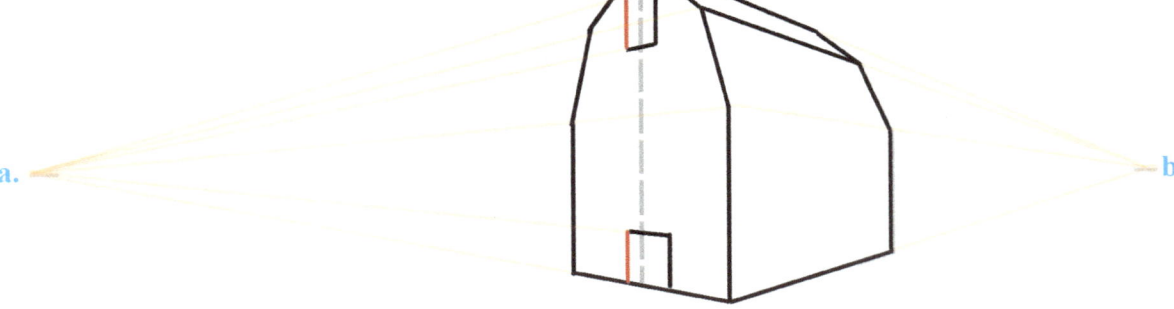

14. Connect the top and bottom of each door with two vertical lines.

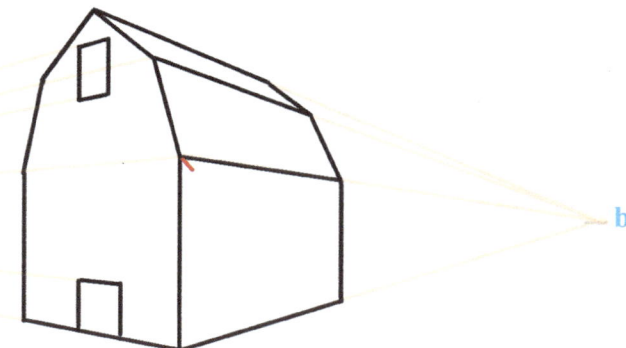

a.   b.

15. Draw a small diagonal line from the corner of the roof to make the eave.

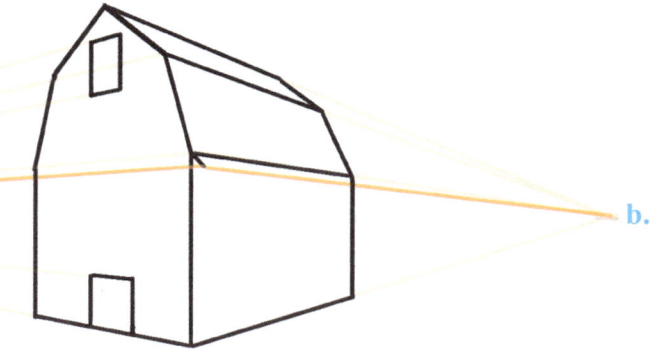

a.   b.

16. Connect **orthogonal** lines from the bottom of that line with vanishing points **a** and **b**.

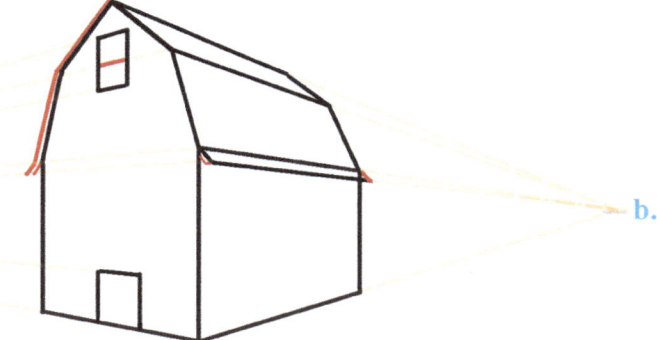

a.   b.

17. Use those lines to add the left side of the roof, a line in the middle of the top opening and the rest of the eave. Erase the extra **orthogonal** lines.

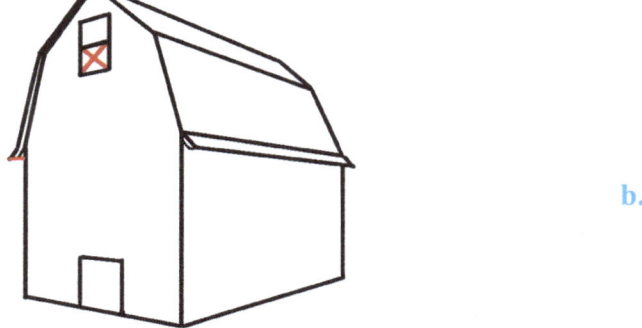

a.   b.

18. Draw an X in the top opening. Draw a line from the left eave to vanishing point **a** and last, erase the extra **orthogonal** line!

45

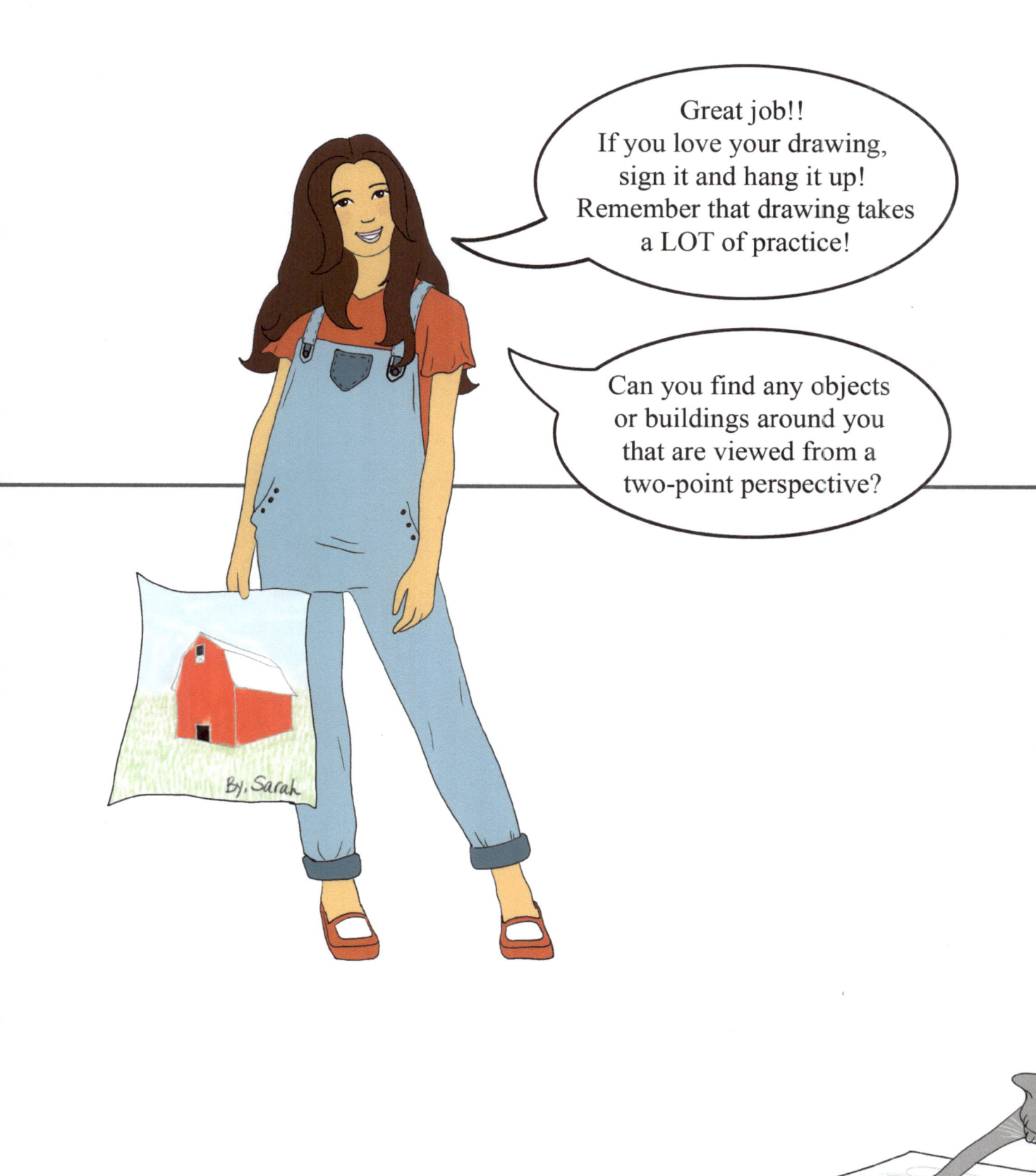

Index

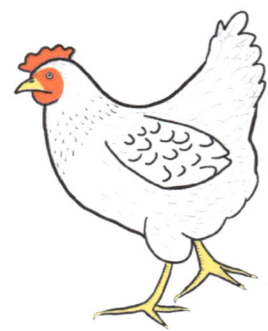

Collect them all!

Visit: IHeardYouCanDraw.tumblr.com

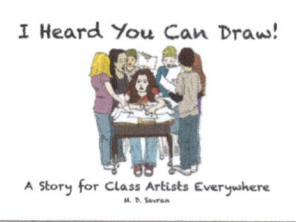

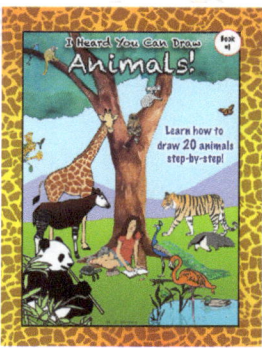 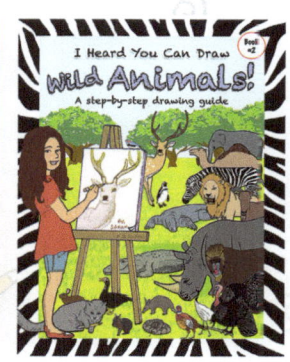 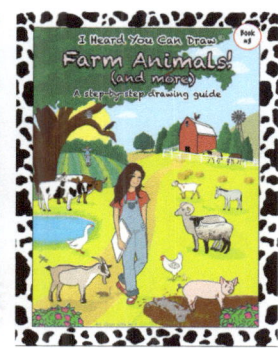

I Heard You Can Draw!
A Story for Class Artists Everywhere
40p Paperback
A picture book about a girl who loves to draw. She discovers how to follow her heart after classmates find out that she has this special talent.

I Heard You Can Draw Animals!© (Book #1)
I Heard You Can Draw Wild Animals!© (Book #2)
I Heard You Can Draw Farm Animals!© (Book #3)

Artist Sketchbooks

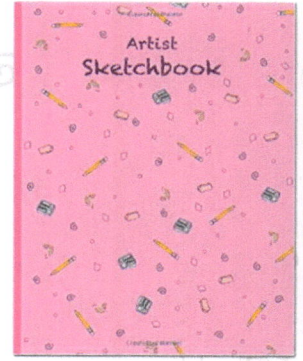 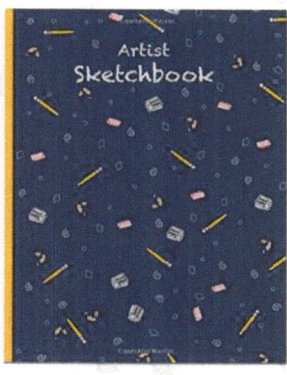 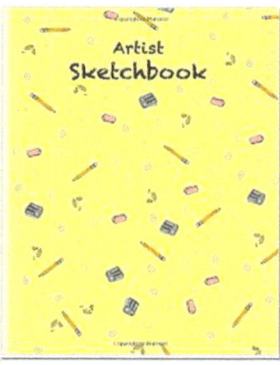 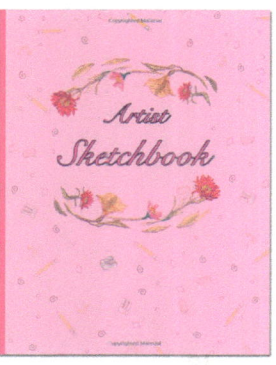

Pink / Navy / Yellow / Pink Flower
60 blank pages

Art Class with Ms. S. Books

www.ingramcontent.com/pod-product-compliance
Lightning Source LLC
Chambersburg PA
CBHW050813180526

45159CB00004B/1648